Sexuality and Modern
Western Culture

Twayne's Studies in
Intellectual and Cultural History

Michael Roth, Editor
Scripps College and the Claremont Graduate School

Other Titles

Anarchism
Richard D. Sonn

Darwinism
Peter J. Bowler

Dissent and Order in the Middle Ages: The Search
for Legitimate Authority
Jeffrey Burton Russell

The Emergence of the Social Sciences, 1642–1792
Richard Olson

Liberalism Old and New
J. G. Merquior

Renaissance Humanism
Donald Kelley

Romanticism and the Rise of History
Stephen Bann

SEXUALITY
AND MODERN
WESTERN CULTURE

Carolyn J. Dean

Twayne Publishers • New York
London Mexico City New Delhi Singapore Sydney Toronto

Sexuality and Modern Western Culture

Carolyn J. Dean
Twayne's Studies in Intellectual and Cultural History Series, No. 8
Copyright © 1996 by Carolyn J. Dean

Library of Congress Cataloging-in-Publication Data

Dean, Carolyn J. (Carolyn Janice), 1960– .
    Sexuality and modern western culture / Carolyn J. Dean.
        p.   cm.—(Studies in intellectual and cultural history)
    Includes bibliographical references and index.
    ISBN 0-8057-8615-5 (cloth)
    1. Sex customs—History.   2. Sex customs—United States—History.
    3. Sexuality in popular culture—History.   4. Sex and history.
    5. Sexology—History.   I. Title.   II. Series: Twayne's studies in
    intellectual and cultural history.
    HQ16.D359   1996
    306.7'.0973—dc20   96-4764
                                                                                          CIP
The paper used in this publication meets the minimum requirements of American National Standard for Information Sciences—Permanence of Paper for Printed Library Materials. ANSI Z3948–1984. ⊗ ™

10   9   8   7   6   5   4   3   2   1   (hc)

Printed in the United States of America

For Susie

Contents

Acknowledgments	ix
Foreword	xi
Introduction	xiii
1. Sexuality, Gender, and Selfhood	1
2. The Development of Sexology	18
3. Sexuality, Gender, and Selflessness	32
4. The Sexual Revolution	46
5. Sexuality, Obscenity Law, and Violence in the United States, 1950–1994	63
Chronology	99
Notes and References	103
Selected Bibliography	120
Index	133

Acknowledgments

The idea for this book grew out of a discussion with Michael Roth. I thank him for nurturing the idea and helping to clarify my thinking over the course of various drafts. I would never have been able to complete the manuscript so quickly without the help of research assistants Gabrielle Friedman, Rachel Gordon, Pamela Swett, and especially Kathryn Schulz. Finally, Margaret Dornfeld of Twayne Publishers offered valuable editorial assistance.

A sabbatical leave from Brown University allowed me to complete the book on time, and friends, colleagues, and students made writing a wonderful task. I cannot possibly thank them all here. I do, however, wish to single out Martin Jay and Lynn Hunt for their continued support, and Volker and Marion Berghahn for being present in so many important ways. I am also thankful to Susan Bernstein and Laurie Bernstein, but my deepest gratitude goes to Susan Schmeiser.

Foreword

Twayne's Studies in Intellectual and Cultural History consists of brief original studies of major movements in European intellectual and cultural history, emphasizing historical approaches to continuity and change in religion, philosophy, political theory, aesthetics, literature, and science. The series reflects the recent resurgence of innovative contextual as well as theoretical work in these areas, and the more general interest in the study of ideas and cultures. It will advance some of the most exciting work in the human sciences as it stimulates further interest in cultural and intellectual history. The books are intended for the educated reader and the serious student; each combines the virtues of accessibility with original interpretations of important topics.

Carolyn Dean's book explores one of the newest and most promising, yet also one of the most amorphous fields of inquiry in the humanities and social sciences. Everyone knows that sexuality is important for diverse groups of people in the West, but there are deep debates about why that is so and how this importance has been constructed (and by whom). Dean's book analyzes the emergence and development of sexuality in North American and Western European cultures from the end of the nineteenth century until our own time. According to her account, sexuality was "created" in the West at the intersection of our representations of the body and of the self, and we now tend to understand both in terms of their relation to sexuality.

Dean concentrates on the transformation of sexuality in the modern period, and its changing role in relation to gender, politics and culture. Sexuality has become one of the primary ways in which we make sense of who we are and what we do, and this book shows how that happened in the last 100 years. Recent debates over pornography in the United States are examined to show how late–nineteenth-century fears of deviance and of the feminine continue to haunt our thinking about representing sex.

Authors writing about sexuality often seem to feel the necessity of choosing between historical research and theoretical discussions of desire. This book's combination of empirical research, theoretical sophistication, and historiographical contextualization makes it a challenging and rewarding example of how cultural and intellectual history can be powerfully combined in the service of illuminating a complex topic of pressing moral, political, and aesthetic concern.

Michael S. Roth
Scripps College and the
Claremont Graduate School

Introduction

A book about "sexuality and modern Western culture" encompasses an infinite number of questions and an endless array of sources. Its focus is difficult to define not just because sexual practices and their meanings shape all aspects of Western historical experience, but because, since the middle to late nineteenth century, our very identities have been inseparable from what we call "sexuality." In other words, the history of modern sexuality is nothing less than the history of changing constructions of the modern self—our changing experiences of ourselves as specific kinds of people. Our interest in matters sexual—whether other people's sexuality, pornography, censorship of sexual images, self-help books—is inseparable from our interest in defining ourselves as unusual or "normal" people.

Sexuality has become a measure of the extent to which one does or does not conform to cultural ideals of selfhood, which invariably reflect the dominance of white middle-class institutions and thus of a male-dominated heterosexuality. Of course, the regulation and production of sexuality is complex and by no means simply mirrors the interests of white middle-class heterosexual men. Nevertheless, their socioeconomic and cultural domination shapes the parameters within which other struggles to define sexuality have taken and still take place.

Sexuality has thus become one of the primary ways in which we define our intelligibility, our identity, our experience—both private and public—of who we are. It is now so all-encompassing and complex a subject that the historian Jeffrey Weeks has declared that its history has no proper focus.[1] After all, what is a sexual activity? Does it always involve another person, and does it always involve bodily contact? Moreover, scholars trying to think about sexuality in the modern period are immediately confronted by a confusing and complicated terminology. "Sex," for instance, refers to many things, and it is only recently that all of its various meanings have been subsumed under the rubric of "sexuality." The word *sex* can literally describe one's anatomy or it can describe activities whose status as "sex" is often uncertain.

The controversy over the meaning of sex is perhaps best reflected in my choice of the word *sexuality*, which presumes that the way we understand sex is inseparable from its cultural meanings. Although we tend to take our anatomy for granted, being a man or a woman means different things at different times and shapes the body's experience of its desires in complicated ways. Similarly, we give sexual practices all kinds of meanings—productive, deviant, sinful, healthy, liberatory, and so on. Otherwise, they would be benign physical activities rather than sites of regulation and anxiety.

Sexual pleasure is thus not a transhistorical natural instinct. I do not mean to imply that sex has no basis in biology but to suggest that biology itself is inextricable from cultural meaning. After all, the use of the word *hormone* to define the workings of "sex chromosomes" did not occur until 1904, but that discovery legitimated sexual differences in supposedly scientific terms that are only now being criticized. In this book I conceive sex as sexuality. I presume sexuality is coterminous with the multifarious social, psychological, and economic structures we loosely refer to as culture.

Many historians of sexuality imply that sex is something authentic or natural or good. Paul Robinson, for example, eloquently celebrates sexual liberation because it subverts "the established organization of society."[2] He insists that our new willingness to understand sex in "businesslike" or scientific terms challenges the rhetoric of moralists who preach what proper sex is and who should be permitted to enjoy it. Robinson thus celebrates the flesh and the spirit at once and in so doing self-consciously articulates a quintessentially modern experience of sex as a spiritual union—an emotional and intimate bond—deeply rooted in the pleasures of the flesh. The Victorians controlled their fear of the body by strictly regulating the forms of its sexual expression. What Robinson calls "sexual modernism," however, now combines emotional intimacy with a joyous attitude toward the body's needs and desires. In short, in liberating the body, we also liberate the spirit.

Robinson's 1976 account remains the predominant paradigm of sexuality in our culture, though it has since been challenged. Yet his moving celebration of the body's pleasures makes very explicit the extent to which we cannot divorce sex from its changing historical meanings. The question we must continue to ask thus concerns how sexual practices come to be invested with particular meanings and why and how those meanings change. For example, recent histories of the family make it clear that sex cannot be confined to the history of marriage and reproduction. These histories explore the changing meanings of the relationship between procreative sex and the institutions (marriage, the state) that produce and regulate it, but they also demonstrate that sex often occurs outside of marriage and not always for procreative purposes. We now know much about changing family forms, but in spite of new kinds of evidence, we still know little about how those forms shape or are shaped by changing heterosexual practices.

Many histories of the family still focus more on the origins and outcomes of structural shifts—for example, industrialization leading to women's migration to the cities and a higher rate of illegitimate children—than on the cultural meanings of sexual expression. As more and more family histories demonstrate, sex is not simply a statistical variable but means different things to different social groups and genders.

Likewise, discussion about sexuality and sexual identities has proliferated since the midnineteenth century, and efforts to historicize sex have involved the investigation of changing attitudes to what constitutes sexual practice itself, as well as an analysis of why some practices are deemed more acceptable than others. Prior to the 1970s a generation of historians presumed the fundamental objectivity of the sexual science they investigated and sought to correct its evident biases—as if sexuality could be examined shorn of its cultural meanings, as if sexuality expressed a transhistorical truth that an unbiased observer might discover. Furthermore, feminist historians and theorists have argued persuasively that sex cannot be neatly separated from gender—from cultural expectations of what it means to be a man or a woman—and that the history of sexuality is necessarily the history of the changing relationship between sex and gender. In other words, any study of sexuality involves both private experience and public debate: it must traverse different classes, races, and genders and situate itself at the intersection not only of diverse cultural groups but of broad historical patterns (for example, the demographic data shaping the definition of families) that impact and mold relations among these groups.

The most influential theoretical effort of recent years is the first volume of the historian Michel Foucault's groundbreaking work *The History of Sexuality* (published in France in 1976; English translation 1978).[3] He argues implicitly that sexuality is inseparable from definitions of selfhood. His book has entirely redirected historical and other scholarship about sexuality and requires some detailed explication, for it is a difficult but influential text that forms the fundamental reference of almost all recent work on modern sexuality.

Foucault's aim was to depart from that other great theorist of sexuality, Sigmund Freud, as well as from almost all received ideas about sex transmitted to us since the nineteenth century. He took issue with the idea that sex is repressed libidinal energy and instead suggested that it is never separable from culture. "Sex" is not an "instinct" acted upon, shaped, or channeled by the environment, the force within ourselves that the Victorians repressed during the last century; instead, Foucault refers to sex as "sexuality." By calling sex sexuality, though, Foucault meant something different from what was intended by the French, German, and British medical men and writers who began to use the term descriptively (and for the first time in reference to human beings) in the nineteenth century.[4]

The late nineteenth–century sexologists, whose early work was best embodied by Richard von Krafft-Ebing's monumental encyclopedia of perversions, *Psychopathia Sexualis* (1886), used sexuality to define selfhood by classifying and categorizing libidinal energy and its diverse forms (for example, homosexuality, sadomasochism).[5] Unlike Freud and his medical predecessors, Foucault did not believe these classifications represented an objective account of the libido's workings; he conceived of them as manifestations of modern sexual regulation. He argued that, by the eighteenth century, sexual regulation no longer simply entailed fostering and preserving alliances— through marriage and reproduction—meant to legitimate and extend paternal sovereignty. Sex was central to the life and death of nation-states dependent on the regulation and maintenance of healthy populations. Lawmakers and other professionals began to develop medical and statistical norms aimed at defining ideal sexual behavior—heterosexual, hygienic and restrained—best suited to capitalist demands for productive workers. Demography, medicine, and pedagogy formed these "technologies of sex" to discipline, shape, and regulate sexuality in the interest of the power of ruling elites.

Most important, technologies of sex did not repress and regulate the intrinsic sexual drives of lazy, pleasure-bound, inefficient bodies but produced those bodies in the interests of the power whose aims they served. Technologies of sex produced normal and abnormal individuals, and the new science of sexology simply represented the increasing differentiation of human beings along those lines. Sexual desire instead differentiated classes, genders, races, and finally individuals, defining who they were and describing what their personalities, thoughts, and behaviors were like. For example, at the end of the nineteenth century sexologists did not discover perverts once neglected by medical science—the homosexual, the sadist and masochist, the fetishist, and so on—but invented them in order to rationalize the regulation of populations in the interest of social order.[6]

In sum, Foucault criticized our assumption that the history of sexuality is the history of a repressed, natural instinct. That assumption, he argued, was born of the Victorian middle class's effort to nurture and create a specific, symbolic "sexual body" in its own image, one that has been given intellectual and cultural respectability by medical professionals, social workers, psychoanalysts, and others since then. The bourgeoisie's belief that sex has to be repressed reflected its efforts to manage and protect normative bodies and populations.

Although I am indebted to Foucault's conceptual framework, I have no intention of defending or challenging his work, a far too ambitious task. Nor will I seek to prove, as some historians have, that many Victorians led fulfilling sexual lives that went against the grain of socially prescribed norms. This argument begs the question of how those norms were constructed and therefore what "sexual fulfillment" means and why it means what it does.[7] Instead, I attempt to offer a coherent account of the history of sexuality by analyzing cultural elites'—legislators, journalists, doctors, critics, and others—complicated efforts to link sexuality to fixed gender identities in Western Europe and North America since the late nineteenth-century.[8] These elites' perceptions of gender roles shaped the meaning of sexuality and defined its relationship to self-formation. I intend to show how their efforts to define sexuality in accord with normative models of healthy masculine and feminine bodies shaped and transformed the image of the restrained, impermeable, rational self central to Western culture since the Enlightenment. I also speculate about why and in whose interests those transformations were effected.

The book thus recounts efforts to fix the relationship between the self, gender, and sexuality since about 1860. Although I focus on the extraordinary power of legislation, popular culture, and diverse media to regulate the relationship between these three concepts, I also emphasize the failure of that regulation in order to explain changing constructions of sexuality—especially the erosion of a coherent, fixed understanding of the "sexual instinct." In particular, I look at female sexuality, homosexuality, and obscenity over time in order to illustrate how sexuality becomes an increasingly fluid concept. More generally, then, this book suggests that sexuality is produced by and understood through the changing intersection of historically specific conceptions of the self and gender.

Although questions about the formation of sexuality must be filtered through particular meanings of race—and issues of gender through the meanings of class and race and so forth—this book privileges gender as a category of analysis. I focus on how gender difference undergirds other social relations where such discussion is relevant: but above all, the relationship between the gendered self and sexuality defines the conceptual center of this text and necessarily determines the material analyzed.

The first two chapters review recent debates in the history of sexuality and lay the conceptual and empirical groundwork for what follows. They focus on the unraveling of the Victorian construction of womanhood and its impact on ideas about sexuality and selfhood. Chapters 3 and 4 concentrate on the interwar years and on how cultural elites restored traditional concepts of gender difference by redefining the relationship of sexuality to the self. Chapters 1 and 3 establish broad themes and contexts, and chapters 2 and 4 elaborate these themes in more specific discourses—in particular, sexology and the sexual revolution.

The final part of the book quickly brings the analysis up to date, focusing specifically on post–World War II America, where recent debates about obscenity legislation have recast earlier themes in new terms. Since the previous discussion focuses more heavily on Western Europe than on North America, the analytical function of this last section is to provide a highly focused, narrow case study documenting the validity of the argument made about the history of sexuality in a closely related and yet quite different context. I hope the reader is persuaded of its significance. The narrowing of the book's focus, in short, shows in very precise terms the crucial changes and continuities in the recent history of sexuality in modern Western culture.

1

Modern Sexuality, Gender, and Selfhood

> What is peculiar to modern societies, in fact, is not that they consigned sex to a shadow existence, but that they dedicated themselves to speaking of it *ad infinitum*, while exploiting it as the secret.
>
> —Michel Foucault, *The History of Sexuality Vol. I*, p. 35.

Since the publication of *The History of Sexuality* in 1976, a number of historians have nuanced Michel Foucault's proposal that modern sexuality dates from the late eighteenth century. Drawing their evidence from local contexts, these scholars have suggested that an important shift in the history of sexuality occurred toward the end of the nineteenth century. But as yet this more specific periodization has not been incorporated into any larger conceptual framework. This incorporation is the project the rest of this book undertakes.[1]

Of course, no historian would deny that the "regime" of sexuality shifted after the Enlightenment and the French Revolution. Even before the Revolution, Enlightenment *philosophes* rejected the metaphysical and religious foundations of the old monarchical order. Challenging the authority of the Catholic Church, these thinkers saw no necessary connection between sexual desire and reproduction, and they refused to condemn the pursuit of sexual pleasure for its own sake, whether within marriage or outside it. Sodomy, a legal category used to cover a wide range of sexual practices, including homosexual relations and bestiality, was stricken from the lawbooks in France in 1791, in the Netherlands in 1811, and even in Bavaria in 1813. These changes did not necessarily reflect more tolerant views of homosexual relations or masturbation (although no longer condemned, such practices were still considered undesirable), but they did repudiate the Church's interference in the vagaries of sexual desire.

A number of historians and literary theorists have observed that during this period attitudes toward gender and sexuality shifted in response to the social and cultural disruptions produced by capitalist development. As manhood came to be defined by an ability to cope with the stresses and strains of modern industrial work patterns, materialism, and urbanity—the "public" sphere—womanhood was more and more equated with the comfort of home and hearth—the "private" sphere. In the late eighteenth and early nineteenth centuries, European middle-class culture idealized domesticity, nature, and hence the intimacy and emotional needs associated with femininity. Within this Romantic "ideology of domesticity," as Thomas Laqueur has argued, women were no longer considered inferior versions of men but entirely different from them. Women and men were incommensurable, like apples and oranges.[2]

Foucault noted that as the home and the loving heterosexual couple were idealized, attitudes toward sexuality, already transmuted during the revolutionary era, took yet another turn. Sexual repression for the first time became a marker of social status: the higher one's social status, the more distant from sex and the disease, excess, and lack of control associated with it. Sexual repression, according to Foucault, became the foundation of a new social order no longer tied to "blood"—to birth and alliances—but to ideas of equality and democracy. In Foucault's words, "the bourgeoisie's blood was its sex" (124, 128–29). Thus, sexual repression marked social status in a new world whose moorings in aristocratic lineage had been severed.

Gender ideology provided the vocabulary for this new language of repression. The received wisdom was that the sexual drive was a natural, primitive force that had to be repressed for the good of civilization. Social adaptations of Darwinian and other evolutionary theories of human development represented unrestrained sexuality as an atavism characteristic of less developed beings. Yet if sexual repression was considered a sign of advancement, it was above all *female* sexual purity that was associated with the most highly developed civilizations and defined race and social class in Europe and North America. Likewise, the presumed connection between what one historian has termed an "overdeveloped body and an underdeveloped mind" was represented above all by unrestrained *female* sexuality. Yet this conception was also applied to working-class men and women, to colonized subjects, and, in the United States, to African Americans.[3] In other words, although women's sexuality was the target of most discussion and regulation, poor and colonized men were discussed, defined, and regulated implicitly as well.

The threat associated with femininity in Victorian culture is most readily apparent in the vast investigations into prostitutes' lives undertaken in the 1830s by British, French, and North American medical men. Alexandre Parent-Duchâtelet, a public health specialist who began his career investigating more efficient means of disposing of sewage and other urban waste, wrote an extremely influential, multivolume work on prostitution in 1836 that set the tone for other works to follow in Britain, North America, and elsewhere.[4] Parent-Duchâtelet defined prostitutes as inferior women with an excessive taste for vice and luxury. He associated them with the more "primitive" sexuality of the working class, from whose ranks most of them came. His obsessive "scientific" investigation into the lives of prostitutes quite literally equated them with sewage.

In the late eighteenth and early nineteenth centuries, efforts were made to criminalize all illicit sex and sexual reading material in order to consolidate bourgeois moral values and in particular to encourage marriage and the cultivation of the private sphere. Surveys often made no distinctions between unmarried women and prostitutes; a 1796 report in London, for instance, exaggerated the number of prostitutes precisely because it included all women without husbands. A large percentage of the female prison population in Boston were women convicted of "nightwalking" and "lewdness." Throughout North America female sexual delinquents were more likely to be institutionalized than men who had committed minor crimes, so that female but not male criminality was increasingly equated with sexual deviance. Indeed, as Barbara Meil Hobson suggests, "sexual deviance" was thought to be "the source of all female criminality" (110). She also argues that the identification of all single working-class women as potential delinquents was part of a larger bourgeois effort to distinguish between the respectable and the unrespectable poor. One by-product of prostitution regulation throughout Western Europe was that all "professional" women came to be seen as less respectable than those who stayed at home.

In the nineteenth century prostitution provoked the same anxiety as the idea of masturbation had during the latter half of the eighteenth century. Male masturbators had been censured for unnecessarily draining their own libido and for lacking self-restraint. Later the medical community believed it was mainly prostitutes who drained men's seminal fluid and thus the productive energy needed to build a new industrial nation. In an economy based on production—and hence, quite literally, on sexual reproduction, on new and healthy bodies—both prostitutes and unmarried women were regarded as a threat to social well-being. Masturbation was still stigmatized, but mainly because it represented the beginning of a slippery slope from the solitary pleasures of boyhood to the "ungovernable passion of manhood"—male masturbators, it was said, always ended up at the brothel (F. le Gros Clark, quoted in Hall, 298).

The "science" that legitimated oppressive legislation during this period cannot be dissociated from white, patriarchal power: it served the interests of bourgeois men by grounding their gender, class, and racial superiority in nature. For example, in the nineteenth century, married, white, middle-class women were "proven" to have brains and skeletons that were docile and slight—in accord with the image of the ideal Victorian woman. Female skeletons, drawn for the first time in the late eighteenth century, had small brains and large hips, presumably to demonstrate women's primary childbearing function.[5]

Throughout this era, *women's* sexuality continued to provide metaphors for class and racial difference. From the late eighteenth century to the end of the nineteenth, novelists, cultural commentators, politicians, and doctors accounted for working-class rebellion in both England and France, for example, by referring to the rebels' atavistic sexuality, and implicitly linked it to unrestrained femininity. In his famous counterrevolutionary treatise, *Reflections on the Revolution in France* (1790), Edmund Burke equated the French Revolution with the triumph of "furies" and "harpies." In 1879 Maxime Du Camp described the 1871 Paris Commune uprising as the unleashing of a frenzied sexuality, symbolized by bare-breasted, monstrous, and drunk female rebels.[6] And Émile Zola's famous 1885 best-seller *Germinal* depicted striking French miners as sexualized and animalized hordes. In perhaps the most famous scene, women workers castrate the owner of the store from which all miners were forced to buy food and other goods.[7]

In North America, meanwhile, slave masters and the majority of white men and women considered African American women intrinsically sexualized and therefore sexually available.[8] In other words, like class difference, racial difference was most often defined in terms of black women's unrestrained sexuality. Although North American, European, and especially imperialist cultural narratives stigmatized both men and women of African descent by reference to their "barbaric" sexuality, in men, this "atavism" was linked to effeminacy. Sander Gilman had argued that in the late nineteenth century, medical men used the Southern African female Hottentot—one Hottentot was exhibited at fairs to voyeuristic European audiences—to symbolize all primitive sexuality.[9]

In myriad texts, moreover, the unrestrained sexuality of prostitutes is described as contagious, irresistible, and destined to undermine the self-restraint that marked the limits of class and respectability. As one historian has written: "The division between the good [that is to say, repressed] and bad [woman] coincided both in theory and in practice with existing class lines."[10] The distinction between good and bad women also represented a more general division between masculinity and femininity, which further enabled, created, and legitimated class—and especially in the United States, racial—divisions.

This function of female identity is significant, for if we understand how gender difference was related to class and race difference, we can begin to explain how transformations in sexuality have been produced throughout its history. That is, the history of sexuality is not simply the history, as Foucault described it, of an expanding disciplinary apparatus that controls and regulates populations; rather, it is a narrative about how (interrelated) racialized, classed, and gendered rhetoric produces sexual subjects in different ways at different times and for different purposes. As a number of theorists and historians have noted, Foucault's work on sexuality almost entirely ignores gender as a category of analysis. As a result, he ignored the central paradox of Victorian culture: that white women's nature was considered at once innately passive (sexually dormant) and innately sexualized (determined by the fluctuations of their reproductive cycles). Femininity thus figured in both woman's inferior or passive sexual drive *and* her body's heightened sexuality.[11]

Victorian physicians believed in a female sexual drive, but they conceived women's sexuality as more limited than men's and as inextricable from their higher spiritual nature. Women's sexual feelings were awakened by dreams of motherhood and spiritual union with the beloved, whereas even the most romantically inspired men had definite sexual needs unrelated to their object of love. Although his view was extreme, the British doctor William Acton, the author of tomes on prostitution and the physiology of sex, wrote in 1857 that "the majority of women . . . are not troubled with sexual feelings of any kind."[12] Even the famous sexologist Havelock Ellis, who did not agree with Acton, noted that the sexual instinct in women was elusive: he meant that it lacked the aggressiveness and urgency of male sexuality (Robinson, 17). Most doctors, Acton aside, were more concerned with the potential intensity of sexual feelings in women than with their perceived sexual limitations, for it was this intensity that divided the "bad" women from the "good."

Thus, Victorian ideals demanded that women exercise the self-control they were also presumed not to possess. Women were conceived paradoxically as both sexually passive and hypersexual: their passivity manifested their superior ability to harness passion in the interest of a higher good, but it also signified their docility, their malleability, the triumph of their bodies' rhythms over their minds—and hence their *lack* of sexual self-control.

Yet medical men never explained why some women became prostitutes or sexual deviants except by claiming that they had "fallen" and hence were morally or physiologically defective. Doctors often conflated nymphomaniacs, prostitutes, and lesbians. They identified unrestrained female sexuality with criminality and disease, even though they could not account for the origin of disease except by making paradoxical references to the sexually passive female body's innately sexualized state. Hence, nymphomania—a term widely used in the nineteenth century to describe all kinds of deviance in women, including masturbation—was tautologically both a cause and a symptom of excessive desire. Nymphomania and prostitution—both forms of female sexual deviance—were like autoimmune diseases: the innately passive female body turned against itself and became sexually voracious.

Doctors similarly neglected to ask why the sexually passive woman would choose another woman rather than a man for a sexual partner. Homosexual women were assumed to be abnormally sexually active (hence their association with prostitutes and nymphomaniacs). Yet it was also assumed that some lesbians remained passive, merely succumbing to the aggressive sexual advances of another. The so-called passive lesbian's decision to give in was most often explained as a temporary aberration encouraged by life in a gender-segregated institution. Her deviant desire was consequently thought to be "acquired"—that is to say, mutable—rather than congenital. Thus, female passivity was often taken for granted—especially in Anglo-American cultures—even in discussions of such "active" aberrations as lesbian sexuality, and female debauchery was assumed to exist even though women were presumably often passionless.

Social Purity Movements and Sexual Regulation

The paradox at the heart of Victorian constructions of sexuality was not unraveled until the late nineteenth century. That unraveling, though impossible to date precisely, coincides with increased attempts to regulate deviance after the 1850s. Such efforts went hand in hand with broader concerns about population control, the management of the colonies, and the restriction of immigration, especially from the East, where Jews were fleeing pogroms in large numbers and flocking to the United States and to western and central European cities, particularly Vienna. Intensified regulation also reflected increased anxiety among elite men about the efforts of women and working-class men to gain political power—and hence about the perceived erosion of gender and class boundaries. Women's suffrage movements, especially in England and the United States, struggled with renewed vehemence to open universities and professions to middle-class women as well as to effect changes in property and inheritance laws. Men everywhere, especially in France, often satirized feminists as "new women" who sought to replace or imitate men. Working-class men also organized effectively on their own behalf, labor strikes were common, and socialist movements gained increasing power, especially in Germany, where membership in the Social Democratic Party (SPD) rose dramatically.

The middle to late nineteenth century also witnessed increasing democratization through literacy, intensified urbanization, technological development, and the fledgling growth of consumer culture.

Though the term "mass culture" would be premature, by the end of the century increased opportunities for upward mobility, the growth of a service sector, and the invention of "leisure time" for the middle class all threatened the hegemony of the male upper class in complex ways.

Between 1850 and 1900, all across Europe and North America, gender boundaries and their complicated cultural association with class and racial superiority began to erode.[13] At the same time the concern with deviance grew more obsessive, and regulatory measures to counteract it increased in severity. The notion of degeneracy—the idea that individuals manifest characteristics that mark them as biologically and hence socially defective—was invented by the French doctor Bénédict-Auguste Morel in 1857 and subsequently gained currency. The term "eugenics," coined by the Englishman Francis Galton in 1883, made a "science" of the elimination of so-called racial impurities and defects. In this discourse on degeneracy, the physical and moral consequences of poverty and immigration were perceived to be inseparable from the demise of the imperial "race" and its mission of cultural and socio-economic expansion. As France and Britain expanded their empires abroad, nationalism became increasingly synonymous with racial purity and virility; medical men were called upon to maintain the nation's fitness and superiority against impurity and emasculation. The regulation of sexuality was regarded as an essential part of this campaign, necessary for the preservation of an imperial race from contamination by "inferior" racial elements. Cultural critics during this period equated such contamination with compromised manhood—the refusal to sacrifice oneself for the national good and the inability to fight. The United States and the imperial powers thus policed sexuality both to maintain the fiction of racial purity and to legitimate white men's racial hegemony. Toward the end of the century, the sexologist Havelock Ellis claimed that "[d]ifferences of race are irreducible" and produce "innately hostile" lovers (quoted in Gilman, 107).[14] In so doing he legitimated imperialist discourses of population control.

In short, medical men and others regulated sexuality in new racial and biological terms in order to reinforce Victorian class and gender hierarchies, as well as to delineate the "white man's burden" as colonial power expanded. These authorities targeted women's and homosexual men's sexual behavior and rhetorically linked the "dilution" of the white race with the nation's emasculation.

In most Western countries, "social purity" movements gained

momentum, attacking prostitution, abortion, homosexuality, and pornography in the name of preserving social order. Drawing on the racialized and gendered rhetoric of medical men and legislators, social purists regarded nonprocreative sexuality as a symbol of industrial nonproductivity. They thus reiterated the well-established associations between sexual excess, loss of virility, and the risk posed by mass culture, which, according to Andreas Huyssen, has "traditionally been described as the threat of losing oneself in dreams and delusions and of merely consuming rather than producing."[15]

In Vienna, for the first time, a detailed policy statement on prostitution was drafted in 1851, and by the end of the century all women incarcerated in that city were registered as prostitutes whether or not they had been arrested for soliciting sex. In Germany prostitution was regulated after unification in 1871, and all states were forced to adopt paragraph 175 of the Prussian penal code, which criminalized "unnatural" acts (specifically, sexual relations between men and bestiality). In Germany and Britain, legislators sought unsuccessfully to extend proscriptions on homosexuality to include women. (Women were included in Austrian laws.)

In France where prostitution had been subject to regulation since the 1840s, criminal laws against nonregulated prostitutes—women who were not registered with the police—were tightened. In North America, because of powerful cultural resistance to the idea of condoning any form of prostitution, regulation (which by its nature assumes that prostitution is a necessary evil) was never seriously attempted except for periods in St. Louis, New Orleans, and San Francisco. Meanwhile, those who engaged in illegal prostitution, as well as those who were suspected of doing so, faced harsher and harsher penalties. Female sexual offenders, especially women of color, began to receive far longer prison terms, and rhetoric warning of the dangers of promiscuous women became increasingly vitriolic.

In Britain, finally, the passage of the Contagious Diseases Acts in 1864, 1868, and 1869 reflected an intensified effort to regulate and control prostitution: prostitutes were forced to undergo medical examinations and to register as prostitutes with the police, even if they walked the streets only to supplement their incomes. In 1885 British politicians passed the Criminal Law Amendment Act (also called the Labouchère Amendment, after its sponsor), which criminalized all male homosexual acts—under the rubric of "gross indecency" rather then sodomy—and raised the age of consent for girls from 12 to 16. (It was under this law that Oscar Wilde would be sentenced to hard labor in 1895.) The Labouchère Amendment was an extension of the 1861 Offences Against the Person Act, which first established an age of consent for girls and criminalized abortion at all stages of pregnancy. The amendment was passed in the midst of fears stirred by increasingly sensationalist accounts of the "white slave trade": innocent girls reportedly were abducted into prostitution by evil procuresses, strange gentlemen, or foreigners.

This melodramatic narrative was most infamously exploited by W. T. Stead's 1885 *Pall Mall Gazette* article, "The Maiden Tribute of Modern Babylon," in which he claimed to have bought a young girl (to expose modern moral evil, he explained). Such stories conflated fears about the uncontrollable and calculating sexuality of prostitutes, debauched aristocrats, and men of color, usually imagined as Turks or Arabs. Legislators passed the amendment in the name of protecting innocent women: in keeping with the paradox that defined Victorian womanhood, the Labouchère Amendment presumed that women's corruption was both the cause and effect of immorality.

As I have argued, "protection" was a double-edged sword: although the amendment appears to punish men for abusing women, by raising the age of consent, restricting reproductive freedom, and penalizing all male homosexual acts, it used unrestrained male lust as a pretext for disciplining deviant women and men, and thus reinforced normative models of manhood and womanhood. By presuming that all women were innocent victims, the law stripped women of sexual agency and continued to stigmatize women who refused to be desexualized. Thus, in the same gesture, legislators protected "good" women and legitimated the punishment of "bad" women who were, as Judith Walkowitz argues, still "blamed for the crimes committed against them" (Walkowit, 1992, 132). Moreover, the law—like Stead's narrative—punished men (primarily homosexuals) and represented male threats to women's honor in the figures of debauched aristocrats and foreigners: men who had repudiated the self-restraint proper to respectable masculinity and behaved like women. In sum, the law effectively displaced responsibility for violence against women onto women and men who manifested dangerous and active—female—sexuality. Politicians thus claimed that regulation protected pure femininity and, implicitly, that uncontrolled femininity had created the need for such regulation.

Similarly, in 1908 British legislators criminalized incest, this time under the aegis of protecting the "race" by protecting its women. In short, most new efforts to regulate sexuality were aimed at controlling the "quality" of the white, middle-class population by controlling female sexuality—that is, shielding "good" women from foreigners and other "inferiors" or exploiters.

It should be remembered that middle-class feminists—most of whom were active in the struggle for women's suffrage—encouraged this ideology of protection while also criticizing the double standard in all systems that regulated prostitution. That is, they denounced regulation on the grounds that by allowing prostitution at all, it legitimated the exploitation of women in men's interests—or in Victorian terms, it legalized "ruining" women for men's pleasure. British feminists, led by the intrepid Josephine Butler, also fought to repeal the Contagious Diseases Act. They found allies among working-class men, who sought to protect working-class women from exploitation by the upper class (though statistically the overwhelming majority of men "serviced" by working-class women were also working-class). Their efforts were successful primarily because they cast their rhetoric in the language of protection.

In North America feminists sought to abolish prostitution on the same grounds; its abolition was part of the platform of the Women's Christian Temperance Union (WCTU) in 1890. In general, feminists sought through the discourse of moral purity and female "passionlessness" to empower themselves by claiming greater moral authority; they did not question the class bias implicit in this discourse. Their perspective was thus easily absorbed by the conservative, paternalist moral rhetoric of the social purity movements in which they participated.

Sexual Regulation and Female Sexuality

In 1903 the success of the Austrian Otto Weininger's *Sex and Character* indicated that "the notion that [respectable] women were passionless was crumbling" (Hobson, 185). Weininger argued, in fact, that women were exclusively sexual beings and inferior to men for that reason.[16] Havelock Ellis and other medical men shifted gears and proposed that both partners in lesbian relationships were sexually active. Even more dramatically, in many narratives, the erosion of a clear distinction between "good" women and prostitutes became increasingly explicit.[17]

As historians Judith Walkowitz and Angus McLaren have shown, by the end of the nineteenth century invective against prostitutes, through much publicized criminal cases like the "Jack the Ripper" murders, no longer shored up class divisions as neatly as it had earlier. Victorian rhetoric had once implied a distinction between guilty and innocent victims of (especially sexual) crimes, reassuring middle-class women that "good" behavior guaranteed their safety. That distinction had become blurry, however, if only because such criminal cases rhetorically and pragmatically had the effect of frightening and controlling *all* women who ventured out alone or in public (Walkowitz 1992, especially pp. 191–228).[18]

Nineteenth-century police roundups of prostitutes frequently did not distinguish between prostitutes and single working women. Even (horrified) middle-class women were occasionally arrested in these forays. The message was that all women were somehow suspect, that all women not under the aegis of male protection made themselves vulnerable to social stigmatization at best and murder at worst. Regardless of class markers, women's sexuality was deemed threatening and in need of control.

Increasingly, not just single working women but married and prosperous women became the object of anxiety and surveillance. For example, medical reports emphasized that abortion was now procured more often by "respectable" women than by prostitutes or the disreputable poor. In 1898 the Michigan Board of Health estimated that "good" women accounted for 70–80 percent of those who sought abortions. In fact, by the early 1880s almost all North American states had already enacted harsh antiabortion laws.[19]

Middle-class women were seeking abortions in increasing numbers because of the pressures of upward mobility and the resultant need to control family size. Yet abortion was rhetorically construed as a crime "against nature." Doctors discarded the older language of "quickening"—which legitimated abortion up until roughly the third month of pregnancy, when the fetus's movements begin to be felt—in favor of punitive rhetoric: women who sought abortions were literally "murdering" their children. This new punitive attitude reflected anxiety over women's increased demands for autonomy and equal education in a period of declining middle-class fertility. Antiabortion rhetoric was aimed at all women, but most discussion focused on middle-class women who, in seeking abortions, crossed the line that differentiated them from their working-class counterparts. Meanwhile, the relative fertility of the working class, which included immigrants and many African Americans, threatened to dilute the quality of the nation's "blood." Most anti-abortion talk thus invoked and demonized the now-suspect "good wife." Because doctors were not particularly concerned with preserving working-class and other populations deemed racially inferior, abortion was repudiated or advocated primarily as a means of population control. Feminist arguments about women's right to control reproduction were often subsumed by this eugenic emphasis.

Obscenity and Homosexuality

Finally, the contemporaneous crackdown on male homosexuality and pornography represented an effort to restore gender boundaries by controlling a presumably contagious and yet covert femininity. Working-class men and all women were defined as vulnerable populations easily lured away from their social duty. The category of "obscenity" was used in the midnineteenth century to permit the control of texts and images that had become available to these most susceptible members of the population.

In 1857 the French writers Gustave Flaubert and Charles Baudelaire were put on trial for works that outraged morality and religion. Flaubert was acquitted and Baudelaire condemned—he was fined, and six of his poems were banned. That same year Lord John Campbell engineered the passage of the Obscene Publications Act, which was clarified in the 1868 case *Regina vs. Hicklin*: in judging an anti-Catholic pamphlet to be obscene, Lord Chief Justice Alexander Cockburn defined specifically the test of obscenity: "whether the tendency of the matter charged as obscenity is to deprave and corrupt those whose minds are open to such immoral influences, and into whose hands a publication of this sort may fall."[20] In 1888 Émile Zola's British publisher, Henry Vizetelly, was sentenced under the act to three months in jail for selling an expurgated version of *La Terre*.

Obscene publications included, significantly, not only sexually explicit images but information about contraception and abortion. In England, for example, Annie Besant and Charles Bradlaugh were prosecuted in 1877 (and acquitted on a technicality) on the grounds of obscene libel for reprinting an American pamphlet that contained information on birth control. The infamous American Comstock Law, passed in 1873, forbade the mailing of obscene art and literature and all material about controlling reproduction.[21] French laws passed in the 1880s similarly classified contraceptive literature, and even pacifist literature, as obscene. In 1904 the Reichstag Commission in Germany declared "smut" a psychic danger to the population.

Both pornography and homosexuality were described over and over again as pervasive and invisible contagions or viruses threatening the health of the social body and leading to the emasculation of the (imperial) nation. In the wake of a series of scandals from 1907 through 1909 in which Kaiser Wilhelm II's entourage was accused of homosexuality, the foremost anti-Semitic politician in the German Reichstag linked the ostensible rise in homosexuality to women's emancipation and the spread of pornography.[22] Evidently upper-class heterosexual men were presumed to be more immune to pornography's contagion, for legislation penalized expensive books less severely than cheap prints and pamphlets.

Max Nordau's 1892 popular treatise on *Degeneration* nevertheless called all men who wrote or consumed pornography "masochists" and "eunuchs."[23] Others likened pornography readers to opium users, drawing on a Western fantasy of a feminized and debauched "Orient" whose populations spent more time in opium dens than at hard work. Pornography, one writer warned, drew out men's feminine character, even turned them into inverts.[24] The consumption of pornography and the existence of male homosexuality in effect threatened to feminize the general population. Social purists' attacks on prostitution, abortion, homosexuality, and pornography at the end of the century were thus not simply attacks on increased democratization cast as efforts to control the presumed immorality of working-class men, nonwhites, and (especially "fallen") women; they were attacks on the erosion of class and gender hierarchies and hence assaults on an uncontrolled and uncontrollable femininity.

The Erosion of Gender Ideology

Women's sexual repression no longer guaranteed the distinction between classes and races, for women had come to be seen as both absolutely pure and absolutely impure and untrustworthy. That is, the Victorian paradox was no longer an unquestioned, if incoherent, social given but a social problem. When they sought to regulate class and racial hierarchies by regulating women's and homosexual men's sexuality, social purists and others called into question women's sexual passivity by making all women and men potential sexual deviants. By casting their nets so wide, by intensifying suspicion, purists imagined a world in which social hierarchies had become increasingly unstable. In this sense their anxieties were quite historically specific and were shaped by real fears of democratization.

For the middle-class men and women active in social purity movements, the democratic world was a nightmare in which it was difficult to distinguish those who slipped down the slope from self-restraint into unproductive expenditure from those who did not. It was no longer so clear who were the good women and who the untrustworthy ones; which of the poor were respectable and which were not; who was a real man and upright citizen and who was a homosexual. This lack of delineation, I have argued, was already implicit in the paradox whereby women represented both self-restraint (sexual passivity) and unproductive expenditure (licentiousness). Once social purists questioned women's natural self-restraint, they undermined the entire rhetoric through which female sexual passivity and purity had supported class and racial divisions, and hence class and racial superiority.

Sexual Secrets and Sexual Subjects

As mentioned earlier, there were other markers of the erosion of gender ideology: the perceived population crisis in competitive, imperialist nation-states with declining birth rates; urbanization; the crisis of faith in democracy evidenced by the emergence of proto-fascism; and the challenges to the status quo by labor organizing and women's suffrage movements. But one of the most important, and usually neglected, signs of this change was a deterioration of the boundaries between moral (properly masculine or properly feminine) and immoral (improperly feminized) individuals—effected above all by the new inability to demarcate good from bad women.

The blurring of previously clear social divisions by democratization led to a new preoccupation with what might be termed the sexual secret. Arnold Davidson describes a new interest in sexual deviance in these terms: "The more details one has about these anomalies, the better one is able to penetrate the covert individuality of the self."[25] That is, men and women were now perceived to have covert identities that doctors could reveal by detecting perverse sexual inclinations. This distinction between real and false identities was hardly new. Victorians had always defined an unblemished moral reputation as the reflection of one's public principles in one's private life, thus implicitly drawing a line between appearance and reality. Yet now a new emphasis had been placed on the private half of this dichotomy. It was above all one's sexual secrets that were supposed to reveal one's true self.

As penalties for both homosexuality and abortion increased in the late nineteenth century, so, too, did the practice of blackmail. In fact, it was during this period that blackmail developed its modern form: threatening to reveal damaging information about someone's private behavior. (Formerly, blackmail had generally involved a threat of physical violence as a defense against exploitation. The threat might be made by an individual, or by an entire community, against a landowner.) The French writer Leo Taxil noted that prejudice against male homosexuals made them easy prey for blackmailers.[26] And in Robert Louis Stevenson's famous *The Strange Case of Dr. Jekyll and Mr. Hyde* (1886), now often read as a novel implicitly about male homosexuality, Jekyll's associates propose blackmail (his lawyer fears the money Jekyll leaves to Hyde was bequeathed to avoid "disgrace") as the most likely explanation of the relationship between Jekyll and Hyde (p. 14). In other words, Stevenson suggests that blackmail provided the culturally dominant interpretation of otherwise incomprehensible behavior.

The sexual secret was constructed as equivalent not just to a covert individuality but to a covert *femininity*—homosexuality (and hence self-indulgence) in a man, excess in a woman. In the late nineteenth–century imagination, sexual identity, and therefore identity in general, was not always assumed to be clearly visible and marked; rather, it had to be ferreted out, read and interpreted. The French doctor Georges St. Paul remarked that homosexuals were an "invisible" population.[27] Other doctors, we recall, noted that the married women who procured abortions were difficult to distinguish from "good wives." Regulation directed at prostitutes, homosexuals, and pornographers, meanwhile, sought to detect and control the pervasive femininity attributed to these radically different social groups.

It was above all the sense of instability that distinguished this new conception of the individual from those that had gone before.

The late eighteenth–century Gothic sensibility had also recognized a difference between public and private selves. But at that time the moral problems posed by this difference were seen as surmountable. The texts of this period may have evinced a fascination with immorality and the fragility of reason, but they usually revealed who the killer was, explained who was good or bad, and demonstrated that reason triumphed over evil. A century later even the (often complex) resolutions offered by Gothic works were no longer viable.

Late nineteenth–century doctors and cultural critics talked as much about sex as earlier Victorians had, but unlike their predecessors, they invented sexuality as a social problem whose manifestations signaled the erosion of Victorian ideals. For them, the world was no longer divided between good (repressed) and bad (promiscuous) women, between indulgent (masturbators) and nonindulgent people, all of whom exercised free will (within their intellectual capacities as determined by doctors, phrenologists, and criminologists), and all of whom made some decision about whether to contribute to a presumably humane and prosperous social order. Now, as we will see, the world was peopled by a vast array of men and women whose bodies acted on both volition and compulsion, who were motivated by immoral decisions as well as by irresistible urges, who displayed both masculine and feminine characteristics. Sexuality both defined moral character and marked its unintelligibility.

2

Sexology

I explained to him my condition, and also gave him *Psycho-pathia Sexualis* to read, expressing the hope that by the force of my own will I should become fully and lastingly master of my unnatural impulse.

—Quoted in Richard von Krafft-Ebing, *Psychopathia Sexualis* (1886)

It was not until the turn of the century that sexuality took on its modern incarnation—that is, became the explicit matrix through which other factors such as class and race worked to produce an individual. Again, sexual regulation at this time was not, as Foucault claimed, only an extension of eighteenth-century capitalist development and the disciplinary regime that accompanied it. I suggest that modern sexuality was also born of late nineteenth-century medical men's inability to resolve the incongruity between heterosexual appearance and non-normative sexual behavior, between gender roles and sexual activities. They tried to resolve this incongruity by examining behavior they conceived as sexually anomalous—especially homosexuality. Their failure, I will argue, produced a new conception of the relationship between sexuality and the self.

I will continue my narrative with a description of early efforts to construct a science of sexuality and the context within which such efforts were possible. I will then examine the ways in which, within this science, the discussion of homosexuality offers especially profound evidence of the simultaneous construction and unraveling of the distinctly gendered self. My analysis will focus on how sexuality constituted and was constituted by the tension between the moral and the medical, the social and the individual, and gender and sexual practices, and how that tension transformed modern sexuality into both the core of selfhood and the "lack" of it.

From Sexual Practice to Sexual Psychology

As I have noted, concern about masturbation and prostitution had existed long before the late nineteenth century. The concept of perversion also had earlier roots. In 1843 the Russian physician Heinrich Kaan published *Psychopathia Sexualis*, the book that would become the model for Krafft-Ebing's better-known volume of the same title; in 1849 the French doctor C. F. Michéa wrote an article on "deviations of the sexual appetite." In these works, perversion was defined primarily as a form of moral insanity, provoked most often by neurological or other organic problems.[1]

By the late nineteenth century, however, sexual psychopathology was posing the problem of sexual deviation in new terms. Gert Hekma defines the major elements of this shift: a new tension arose over the problem of whether deviance was a sexual practice or a psychic identity; a new (confusing and inconsistent) vocabulary emerged to define new kinds of deviation; a new classification system replaced that of pathological anatomy, defining symptoms as forms of desire rather than as levels of libidinal "energy"; and finally, a conflict unfolded over whether perversions could be explained in terms of vice (as "perversity") and hence as a moral problem, or in terms of biology (as "perversion") and hence as a physiological problem (178–81). Furthermore, this shift in focus away from sexual practices to the psychology of perversions was consistent with a general transfer of interest from the consequences of acts to their causes, from the description of behavior to a preoccupation with the impulses that drive it.

The Invention of the Sexual Instinct

Fin-de-siècle medical men and their heirs were especially perplexed and intrigued by the subject of perversion because its causes were not at all self-evident. As Arnold Davidson has demonstrated, the notion of a sexual instinct was invented at this time precisely because sexual deviation could no longer be linked to pathological anatomy in any but the most convoluted fashion. The sexual organs of deviants were often observed to be perfectly normal. Finding no evidence of deviance in the sexual organs, physicians looked to the brain to give this new instinct an organic basis, but the brain also failed—as many of them frankly admitted—to reveal the origins of perversion. The idea of a sexual instinct was thus created as a way of circumventing this problem and (falsely) giving the impression that sexual desire and hence its anomalies could be located in the body. Perversions were accordingly redefined as dysfunctions of the instinct, whose normal function was the reproduction of the species.

Davidson argues further that this development represented an "epistemological break" and a new "psychiatric style of reasoning"—the first attempt to link sexuality to selfhood (1990, 295–325). Thus, textbooks now exhibited deviants' facial expressions rather than their anatomy.

Although it would be absurd to deny the power of this new "style of reasoning," it is worth emphasizing that it grew out of a failure to define anomalies of desire in older, more familiar terms. It has never fully replaced the older model, nor has it ever been completely coherent. Thus, the physician Joseph Moreau de Tours claimed that he could find no center or point of origin for the sexual instinct; nevertheless, he was convinced it existed (Davidson 1990, 302). Numerous other examples mirror the tension between old and new models of sexual deviance. For instance, Krafft-Ebing's 1886 *Psychopathia Sexualis*, the model for all other treatises on perversions and a compendium of case studies, sought to determine in each case whether the individual suffered from perversity (a disease of the moral will) or perversion (a disease of the body). The latter diagnosis absolved the pervert of culpability. Dr. Joanny Roux claimed that sexual instinct could not be located and sought to differentiate sexual "need" (discharge) from what he termed sexual "hunger" (the need for love).[2] Many doctors, including Roux, disputed the existence of a "normal" sexual instinct even as they presumed it. Only 3 percent of the population, Roux noted, was "normal as we have come to understand the term."[3] In 1902 the German dermatologist Iwan Bloch, who heavily influenced Freud, published a study on the etiology of perversion in which he demonstrated that so-called sexual aberrations had existed at all times and in all cultures, suggesting that the boundary between normal and pathological behavior varied historically and culturally.

The tension between the old moral or volitional models of deviance and the new biological and compulsive ones arose out of this inability to locate the sexual drive definitively in the body. Roux's differentiation between sexual need and sexual hunger followed the sexologist Albert Moll's famous distinction between two types of sexual instincts or "drives" in his 1897 treatise on the libido. Moll distinguished between "discharge" [*Detumeszenz*] and a "relationship drive" [*Kontrekation*] (cited in Hekma, 182), foreshadowing Freud's 1905 comment in *Three Essays on the Theory of Sexuality* that the sexual instinct is the "psychical representation of an endosomatic, continuously flowing, source of stimulation. . . . The concept of instinct is thus one of those lying on the frontier between the mental and the physical."[4] Freud's formulation, by sundering any clear links between what he later termed the sexual aim (discharge) and the sexual object (whom or what one desires), denaturalized heterosexuality: if the discharge could be effected by any object (opposite sex, same sex, animal or even inanimate object), the drive toward heterosexual reproduction could no longer be deemed instinctive. And further, if the sexual instinct was located at the intersection of body and mind, it was neither solely a product of the body, and hence organic, nor wholly a product of the will, and hence an indulgent "vice" that could be constrained and controlled. That is, the "instinct" was simultaneously experienced as a corporeal "need" and as a "hunger" for someone or something inseparable from this need. Biology and psychological fantasy were inextricably intertwined, leading to the extraordinary possibility that the body's needs (the "natural" sexual instincts) were always also the mind's fantasies. This unresolved tension between mind and body became the cultural fantasy of the meaning of sexuality: sexuality is talked about endlessly because it cannot be clearly defined, because it is always a culturally constructed fantasy about what the body desires.

Late nineteenth–century investigations of male and female homosexuality indicate that this new, less stable (because not clearly "natural") relationship between mind and body troubled the gender norms implicit in the Victorian construct of womanhood. They also demonstrate the extent to which gender boundaries became inextricable from elite men's fantasies about what normative heterosexual relationships should be.[5]

Homosexuality and the Homosexual Rights Movement

The study of homosexuality began in Germany, where it was intertwined with the struggle to eliminate state proscriptions against homosexual practices. The word *homosexual* was coined in an 1868 letter written by Karl Maria Kertbeny criticizing the extension of Prussian proscriptions to the recently annexed German state of Hanover. Later the Eulenburg Affair (1907–1909), in which a journalist accused high-ranking officers around the Kaiser of homosexuality, made the need to explain this "perversion"—responsible for the presumed decline of the German "race"—appear urgent (Hull, 133–34).

Until roughly 1900 the dominant explanation of male homosexuality, proposed by the homosexual lawyer and classicist Karl Heinrich Ulrichs in the 1860s, was that homosexual men had a "woman's soul enclosed in a male body [*anima muliebris in corpore virili inclusa*]" (Hekma, 178).[6] Ulrichs defined male homosexuality as an inborn trait located in the brain (and in his later works, in the testicles). The Berlin psychiatrist Karl Westphal dubbed this phenomenon "sexual inversion" and defined it as a psychopathological condition.[7] This view of male homosexuality was widely influential.

Iwan Bloch, another German advocate of homosexual rights, who corresponded with Havelock Ellis on the matter, was the first to refer to such studies as *Sexualwissenschaft*, or sexology. In addition to his 1902 work on that subject, Bloch wrote an important book entitled *The Sexual Life of Our Time* (1907), in which he extended his earlier anthropological and interdisciplinary approach to the study of sexuality. The first *Journal of Sexology* was published in 1908 by the homosexual rights activist Magnus Hirschfeld, who openly militated against paragraph 175 of the Prussian penal code condemning "unnatural acts" in Prussia and later in all of Germany.

All of these men were indebted to Krafft-Ebing and other predecessors, but at the same time they sought to redirect sex research away from the question of whether "deviants" were sick or "degenerate." Instead, they conceived homosexual desires as variations of a natural drive. The most important advocate of this position was Havelock Ellis, whose six-volume *Studies in the Psychology of Sex* was published between 1897 and 1910. The fourth part of the first volume concentrates almost exclusively on men, focuses on "inversion," and insists on its congenital nature. Ellis, after others, explained that "acquired inversion"—homosexuality as a "learned" behavior manifested most commonly in gender-segregated institutions—is the belated appearance of a congenital disposition.[8] He also insisted that homosexuality was not a disease but was linked to an organic bisexuality latent in all individuals—a theory widely accepted and derived from older notions of hermaphroditism. Ellis sought in some cases to distinguish male homosexuality from gender inversion pure and simple by noting that the sexual invert may have retained some of the gender characteristics of his own sex even while he directed his sexual impulses toward same-sex partners (Ellis did not, however, extend this insight to female homosexuality). In making this distinction, he defined homosexuality more narrowly and could distinguish it from, for example, transvestism (1–64, 75–194, 195–263).

Before and after Ellis, German and other sexologists generally accepted the biological model of sexuality, which rooted homosexuality in a compulsive, congenital instinct. Homosexual rights advocates had good reason to champion this view, for it absolved the homosexual of responsibility for his actions and thus protected him from legal prosecution. The reigning epistemologies of materialism and positivism, moreover, supported such a model. Doctors and others continued to argue about whether and to what extent the instinct was "natural," but by 1901 even Krafft-Ebing ambivalently accepted the idea that homosexuality was not a perversity but a "perversion"—a drive over which the individual had no control.

In 1897 Hirschfeld founded the Scientific-Humanitarian Committee, which maintained that homosexuality was congenital. The committee allied itself with advocates of eugenics on the grounds that marriage was opposed to the true nature of the homosexual and that children conceived by homosexuals would inevitably be unnatural, feeble, and unfit. Hence, members sought rather perversely to harness the eugenic argument condemning homosexuals to arguments for homosexual rights. Although their reasoning was odd, committee members located pathology not in the homosexual's nature but in society's attempts to toy with a "natural" drive.

Adolf Brand (whose marriage and connections with Nazis protected him later from persecution) and Benedict Friedländer founded another homosexual rights group in 1902 called the Community of the Other (or "the Special").[9] They condemned effeminate men and excluded women from membership, insisting that "real" men loved men and that homosexuals were more manly than heterosexual men. Friedländer rejected the idea of a congenital disposition because, as he put it, "one can . . . pity the diseased, one can behave humanely to the sick and . . . try to 'heal' them, but at no time does one acknowledge presumed physical inferiors to have equal rights."[10] If understood as a congenital disposition, homosexuality, he believed, would not be interpreted as a natural drive but would reinforce the disease model. The ensuing history of racism and the more recent quest to determine the biological origins of (male) homosexuality have proven him right, but his solution—asserting the moral superiority and hence difference of the male homosexual—merely reiterated the logic by which homosexual identity could be defined only as similar to or different from heterosexuality, and hence only as either normal or pathological. To destigmatize male homosexuality, homosexuals and sexologists wrenched this logic in creative directions.

Some homosexual rights advocates paradoxically assumed a congenital difference in homosexuals in order to argue for their right to be treated as if they were heterosexual; sexologists who opposed sodomy legislation argued that such a congenital difference should make no difference before the law. Others presumed the moral difference (superiority) of homosexuals in arguing for homosexual equality. Both groups seemed to claim that male homosexuals were fundamentally different from heterosexuals.

Of course, doctors usually explained male homosexual "difference" as a form of psychic femininity. But the cause of such a gender inversion remained obscure. Krafft-Ebing noted that a person's character "correspond[s] with the peculiar sexual instinct," that is, with the "sexual role in which they feel themselves to be," not with their physiological sex.[11] He assumed that gender inversion caused the dysfunction of the sexual instinct while also assuming that the dysfunction of the instinct produced gender inversion. In short, he presumed the dysfunction he sought to explain.

Although Havelock Ellis suggested that gender inversion did not fully explain male homosexuality, (inversion being the medical term for homosexuality) he remained committed to this model to explain female "inverts." Even Ulrichs and Hirschfeld used the term "Third Sex" (Hirschfeld claimed to have borrowed it from ancient Rome), collapsing gender and sexual "inversion." The term's multiple meanings—the androgyne, the "born homosexual," even the "new woman"—conflate male homosexuality with femininity and vice versa. Yet Hirschfeld also insisted that homosexuals had the same sense of honor and shame as ordinary men and were generally indistinguishable from the vast majority of "normalsexuals."[12]

Only Freud, with whom Ellis disagreed, seriously questioned the paradigm of gender inversion (as well as congenital homosexuality) by distinguishing between sexual object and aim. Freud, in contrast to the medical men—Moll, Bloch, and others—who influenced his work, challenged the entire construction of a "sexual instinct" as it had been commonly conceived since Krafft-Ebing. In arguing that the relation between object and aim was the outcome of the struggle he would later term the Oedipus complex, Freud assumed that reproductive heterosexuality was not a natural instinct: instead, it was the product of a successful psychic struggle in which one identified with (and introjected) the same-sex parent. Freud thus called naturalized heterosexuality entirely into question. It was not his intention, however, to discard normative notions of heterosexuality; the healthiest resolution to the Oedipus complex is, of course, procreative heterosexuality (although Freud was not terribly optimistic about even the healthiest "heterosexuals"). Furthermore, because Freud's work would not have its great impact until the interwar period, gender inversion remained the dominant paradigm of male and female homosexuality for many years.[13]

Through their contradictory logic, the early theories of male homosexuality struggled to ascertain the relationship between sex and gender. Sexologists and homosexual rights advocates both insisted and denied that homosexuals were different: if they were morally, emotionally, and (at least in appearance) physically like heterosexuals, how could doctors account for their congenital difference? And if they were not congenitally different, than how *were* they different (or in the case of Brand and Friedländer, the most "manly" men)? These questions became even more urgent when the discussion turned to female homosexuality.

Female Homosexuality

Until recently, lesbians had formed no organized movement on their own behalf, and historians have had difficulty locating primary sources about women who engaged in same-sex relations. With some exceptions, historians have generally included lesbians in larger discussions of the history of homosexuality, which remains primarily a history of men. These historians have rightly conceived the making of the homosexual, and particularly of the lesbian, as a response to threatened gender boundaries. Feminists were often accused of lesbianism, but such accusations were an encoded way of pointing out the more fundamental transgression: such women had left their "proper place" in a society founded on an ideology of separate spheres. Like men who possessed women's souls, women who transgressed normative gender roles, regardless of their sexual practices, were psychically men and hence "inverts."[14]

In contrast to most, if not all, recent historical work on lesbianism, historians have also conceived male homosexuality in terms of public, if often persecuted, sexual subcultures. Homosexual men were persecuted because of their sexual practices, the subcultures they generated, and what both those practices and that presence symbolized. Only recently has lesbianism been discussed in these terms.[15] Middle-class women's gender identity (as well as their supposed moral superiority) had always been defined, at least since the end of the eighteenth century, in terms of their sexual passivity. Documents that do exist from late nineteenth–century German sources reveal that literate lesbians described their desire in spiritual rather than sexual terms, reiterating Victorian norms of womanhood even as they challenged them (Faderman and Eriksson, 1–99). Sexological categories were not merely labels imposed on men and women, as the struggle against proscriptions on homosexuality demonstrates. They were the product of the interaction between individuals with anomalous desires and doctors' interpretations of those anomalies. The men and women addressed by these categories integrated them into more complex, if culturally circumscribed, autobiographies to help explain the inexplicable. Thus, sexology shaped and was shaped by men's and women's reported experience of their sexual deviance.

Lesbians who read Krafft-Ebing were relieved to find the "cause" of their anomaly or "difference" explained. Yet as demonstrated in novels by lesbians and by the political rhetoric of those who participated in Hirschfeld's committee, lesbians did not attribute their difference to homosexuality per se but to their discomfort with prescribed femininity. The little evidence we have suggests that many women who were content with the label "lesbian" or "invert" often did not adopt the implicit judgment in that label. Though few were as confident as the French writer and English ex-patriate Renée Vivien [Pauline Tarn], who in 1904 declared ironically that heterosexuality was unchaste and incomprehensible, most suggested they felt a discrepancy between doctors' views on their "condition"—which often included predictions of suicide or madness—and their own psychic lives[16] (Faderman and Eriksson, 10–11, 27–28, 32–33). The dialectic between sexologists' labels and individuals' lives applied equally to men and women, so that women defined as "lesbians" understood their desire as much in terms of gender norms as gay men did.

The Anglo-American world of "romantic friendships," the absence of public sexual subcultures except in Paris, and the dominant ideology of middle-class women's sexual passivity have made it difficult for historians to document or speak of lesbian sexuality except as gender transgression. Thus, historians have tended—however unintentionally—to replicate late nineteenth–century sexological views of lesbian sexuality as gender inversion. But, as recent works have demonstrated, this notion of lesbianism as solely gender inversion is an extremely reductive reading of efforts in the late nineteenth and early twentieth centuries to come to terms with lesbian desire.

In a recent book about masculinity in modern France until roughly 1914, Robert Nye contends that in that country male inversion was conceived as an inferior form of heterosexual love instead of an equally powerful desire directed at the "wrong" love object (114). Although this conception of male inversion was specific to France, French doctors' perceptions of inverts were similar in important ways to conceptions of male homosexuality elsewhere. That is, homosexual men were conceived as weak, timid, lacking, and hence feminine beings. Nye makes almost no mention of lesbianism, though sexologists were more inclined to attribute female homosexuality to "vice"—that is, to moral turpitude and the apparently irresistible quest for pleasure rather than to congenital instinct. Nye does note that the "weakness" of homosexual men's desire was paradoxically linked to the strength of desire itself, because weak men were more susceptible than strong ones to inappropriate temptation (114–15). Gender inversion expressed the extraordinary irresistibility and power of desire for lesbians as well. But in lesbians, inversion was not linked to weakness; rather, it reiterated received ideas about the insatiability of female desire.

Whereas the homosexual man's susceptibility to pleasure extends the theory of inversion because it expresses his emasculation, the lesbian's desire calls that theory entirely into question: it makes gender inversion both central to explaining the origins of her behavior (the lesbian is sexually active and hence manly) and incapable of doing so (the lesbian is sexually active and hence acting out the presumed excess that characterizes unrestrained femininity). The lesbian is at once a man in a woman's body and an atavistic, depraved woman.

As the French physician L. Thoinot put it in 1898, "You should not be surprised that the inverted woman brings to her love the violent passion she brings to normal love," so much so that in most cases the relationship leads to murder.[17] Thoinot cited the 1892 American case of Alice Mitchell (also cited by Krafft-Ebing), who allegedly slashed her lover to bits with a razor blade after she was forced to leave Alice and marry a man. In fact, Mitchell cut her lover's throat, but Thoinot's extrapolation does replicate a recurrent fantasy about the nature of lesbian love: that it releases the unruly, murderous passion lurking beneath the outward appearance of even the most virtuous woman.

The ancient notion of insatiable female desire was first challenged in the eighteenth century.[18] Yet the new construction of lesbian identity was not simply an extension of an older view. Nineteenth-century medical men sought to make a distinction between disease and vice—between the perversion of the sexually passive female nature, which was innate in the body, and the immoral quest for pleasure, which also represented the innate susceptibility of women to the demands of their bodies. Thus, their conception of lesbianism represented an extension of the paradox by which womanhood was constructed in Victorian culture.

Yet it also unraveled that paradox. The diseased body could not be held morally responsible for its perversion, just as women could not be held responsible for their physical incapacities. The disease marked the female body here as masculine, or "inverted," even as it marked its excesses and passions—in short, its decidedly female nature.

While Dr. Thoinot took pains to make a distinction between what he called "true inversion" and "tribadism" (348), he invented another category that he believed reflected a more accurate picture of lesbianism: "inversion-vice." Thoinot implied that lesbian desire expressed both manliness and womanliness—that is, both the innate and perverse desire to be a man and the excessive pursuit of pleasure symptomatic of unrestrained femininity. This conflation was reflected in European images of prostitutes, who were frequently portrayed as lesbians because they defied women's natural sexual passivity, allegedly engaged in their trade less for money than for love of vice.

In his reading of lesbianism, Dr. Caufeynon similarly charged lesbians with more than gender transgression. Lesbians usurped male prerogative, he argued, and thereby expressed the excesses of femininity: like Sappho and her companions, "their strange tastes make them susceptible to pleasure that only the most exalted imagination could conjure."[19]

When they made these kinds of arguments, medical men were reproducing the image of the lesbian constructed in nineteenth-century literature—both popular literature (especially British flagellation pornography) and middle- and highbrow (primarily French) texts. In fact, Sappho—whose name became a synonym for lesbian identity—was as important a figure as Sade in the late nineteenth–century French literary imagination, and writers and poets from Baudelaire to Swinburne were virtually obsessed with images of lesbian sexuality.[20] During this period Sappho was no longer simply the exceptional intellectual woman, and hence necessarily manly; the lesbian poet of ancient Greece was thoroughly sexualized and transformed into an example of hyperbolized femininity. Images of Sappho, as a poet but above all as a lesbian, proliferated. Flagellation pornography invariably featured a lesbian sadist who dominates the man through her aristocratic reserve while expressing through her punishments an uncontrollable, passionate hatred of men. Hence "Dr. Samuel" describes the flagellant in his pornographic work as a "woman-man."[21]

Obviously, these texts pose many questions and suggest diverse readings. Why, after all, is the female flagellant almost always coded as a lesbian? How do we explain the fascination with the lesbian vampire during this period if not by reference to the dangerous contagion represented by uncontrolled female sexuality, itself symbolized by lesbian sexuality?

My primary point is that, in late nineteenth–century Europe, it was not lesbian desire as gender inversion that dominated medical and literary discourses but lesbian desire conceived as the destabilization of gender boundaries. That is, when the lesbian acts as a sexual aggressor, she expresses masculinity, because she is active and plays the masculine role, *and* a hyperbolized femininity. In their construction of the lesbian, late nineteenth–century medical men so completely blurred the medical and moral categories of illness and vice that the medical origins of illness could be found only in the moral unraveling of the female self.

I cannot fully account for or explain here this construction of and obsession with lesbian sexuality, nor can I address the efforts of some lesbians to turn that construction into a language of their own. Rather, I hope to show that the construction of lesbian sexuality during this period reveals that the "truth" of so-called perverse sexual identity could not be linked to gender norms in any coherent fashion. Medical texts about lesbians reveal myriad contradictions as well as a near-obsession with lesbian sexuality.[22] Medical men, politicians, and cultural critics saw both male and female homosexuality as symbols of social disorder. Nevertheless, they were clearly fascinated with lesbian desire, which threatened to destabilize all established gender boundaries and hence disrupt dominant constructions of normal sexuality.

To review my argument briefly, then, during this period the principles of sexual difference underlying the presumed relationship between mind and body began to erode, and it became increasingly difficult to distinguish between "good" and "bad" women. *All* women were now potential prostitutes and hence potential perverts. And because all women were potential perverts, the line between moral and immoral, public and private, will and compulsion, sex and gender, and, most seriously, between men and women, became increasingly unclear. If women were no longer sexually passive but innately sexualized, what precisely marked their difference from sexually active men? The paradox that defined womanhood was inextricable from the equally paradoxical discourse in which perverts were at once weak-willed *and* driven to perversion by innate disease—by "compulsion." Now all perverts became *like* women, and marked the uncertain status of normative gender roles.

Late nineteenth–century medical men sought to represent the disjunction between public and private selves as the result of a subversive femininity that only their expertise could detect, identify, and define. But their construction of lesbian sexuality demonstrated to what extent they were unable to contain the contradictions in which their investigation of "perversion" was embedded—as evidenced by the myriad contradictions in sexological constructions of the pervert and by the fact that normality itself became an object of scientific inquiry.

The self was now marked by discontinuity between sexuality and gender even as medical men, politicians, and others made broad cultural efforts to sustain some continuity between the two categories of identity. This is not to say that this self represents the failure of nineteenth-century middle-class men to regulate sexuality—their regulation programs were enormously successful, as I have demonstrated. Rather, it represents the outcome of a process whereby their very success was indicative of a crisis of confidence in their power to control female sexuality. Dialectically, the struggle to maintain gender boundaries reconfigures them and, in the process, reconfigures the relationship between sexuality and the self. The story of that continuing struggle is the focus of the next two chapters.

3

Sexuality, Gender, and Selflessness

[Love is] the desire to belong to the self no longer. . . . Love
destroys the personal self and reaches out to the substantial
self. . . . Love saves us from our self.

—Emmanuel Berl, *The Nature of Love* (1924)

In the midnineteenth century, European and American medical
men, legislators, and other authorities increasingly associated sexuality with selfhood, and selfhood with more or less sexually "normal" character types. Increased sexual regulation—and hence
increased controls on the lives of individuals—was inextricable from
the erosion of gender boundaries and the concomitant erosion of
the distinction between will and compulsion on which gendered
(and other) identities were founded. As the need to sustain conventional hierarchies became more urgent, the possibility of doing so
steadily diminished.

In this chapter, I address the ways in which, after World War I
(1914–18), male professionals, intellectuals, and other cultural commentators sought to preserve gender boundaries by transforming
the meaning of heterosexuality. In his 1924 book *The Nature of Love*,
the American writer Emmanuel Berl made heterosexual relations
the privileged means of recovering an authentic, indivisible, "substantial" self presumed to have been destroyed by the ravages of

war, women's emancipation, and materialism. Berl implied that modern individuals had somehow lost their "real" selves, and he linked this loss to "living in a crowded city," to the "shackles of wealth and poverty" that defined identities in socioeconomic terms—and hence to "loneliness," to urbanization and modernization.[1] Moreover, he suggested that the true self can be discovered, paradoxically, only through union with another person.

How and why did white heterosexuality acquire this privileged status? How, in other words, did it become inextricable from what was most authentic about the self? Twentieth-century historians of both western Europe and North America have conceived the interwar years as the beginning of a shift from "homosociality" to "heterosexuality." This shift entailed the transformation of an agrarian, community-based society, in which social relations grew out of extensive kinship networks, into an industrial, urban, and hence mobile society in which social networks were divorced from community. The nuclear family replaced the extended family, and monogamous heterosexual relationships became the primary means of individual fulfillment and social sustenance. Accompanying this development was the gradual replacement of homosocial "separate spheres" by "companionate" marriage, in which men and women ostensibly shared each other's lives as equals in all respects.

Thus, even though Berl's emphasis on romantic love sounds Victorian, it already presumed the significance of companionship in the twentieth-century sense: it looks to heterosexual love as the primary means of repairing self-division and effecting self-restoration in the alienating and fragmented modern world. Berl's mourning of the self and hope that through love it might be rediscovered were quite different from the Victorians' critique of urbanization and its harsh emotional and social consequences. Both middle- and working-class Victorians, albeit from different points of view, also complained of the loneliness produced by the fast pace of capitalist production and of what they perceived as the transformation of human beings into machines. Social purists objected to the conversion of flesh—of "nature"—into a market commodity (prostitution, pornography) as well as to its abasement in the forms of sexual expression produced by the lust and greed they associated with urban environments and cosmopolitanism.

But Berl's view of romantic love was shaped by the consequences of The Great War. That war has often been credited with challenging the class and gender hierarchies of Victorian culture. It also facilitated the unbinding of the paradox that had defined Victorian gender relations. The war rendered traditional marriage increasingly untenable as a solution to the practical and existential problems of desire, loneliness, and isolation. Marriage, of course, remained a durable institution; in fact, marriage rates rose during the interwar period and again in the 1950s. But the character of marriage had changed, for middle-class Americans and Europeans perceived that the Great War had blurred the gender divisions upon which this institution had traditionally been based. The war transformed the meaning of marriage and heterosexuality, and it shapes the way we understand them still.

My task, then, is to demonstrate how and why Victorian gender ideology was no longer perceived to provide an adequate solution for desire, loneliness, and anomie. For loneliness now represented what one recent critic has termed an "incurable" state. Although the condition of being alone had been a feature of the modern self since early Romanticism, in the interwar years—when sexuality could no longer be sublimated, satisfied, regulated, or contained securely within institutionalized boundaries—the self became irreparable.[2] This self-shattering is the loss of the "real" self to which Berl referred.

Women and the Great War

No historian would contest the idea that the Great War effected major social and cultural changes. Its effect on class and race hierarchies is vividly portrayed in Jean Renoir's 1936 film classic *The Grand Illusion*, in which aristocratic officers and ordinary soldiers, Jews and non-Jews, were all forced to live in close quarters under the same material conditions. As many historians have argued, the impact of the war on social hierarchies facilitated the development of "mass culture," a phenomenon born of democratization and expanded consumer capitalism. No less powerful was its influence on conceptions of gender.

Women, of course, did not participate in the war as combatants. Yet as more and more men were sent to die at the front in what was primarily a war of attrition, women were encouraged and expected to take over the war industries. Government propaganda represented working women symbolically as the "home front"— as if the private sphere had been extended to encompass the entire nation. For many middle-class women, the war provided the first opportunity for economic independence, and many white working-class women for the first time were employed at highly skilled, high-paying jobs, from which they had traditionally been excluded. In most European countries, governments provided mothers with economic subsidies to support their families in the absence of a "primary breadwinner." Governments also opened day-care centers and networks of maternal health clinics to provide counseling, advice, and even clothes for women suffering the worst ravages of a wartime economy. In 1917, for the first time, French women were granted primary guardianship of their children. By introducing such measures, governments created bureaucracies and expanded the welfare state, including institutions run by middle-class women acting as social workers and administrators of various sorts. Most of these social policies were not necessarily undertaken for the benefit of women and children but to support the war effort and ensure social order. War propaganda continued to depict women primarily as mothers, wives, sisters, and lovers whose function was to nurture soldiers' psychological and bodily war wounds. Meanwhile, the nation itself was often represented as a woman in need of protection. Yet despite these efforts to offset the expansion of women's roles, it cannot be denied that the war had some positive material consequences for women.

In most western European countries and in North America women gained the vote partly in recognition of their contribution to the war effort. Moreover, because women's service in the public sphere counted as work befitting a citizen (a "public" person), it became harder, although not impossible, to exclude women from full citizenship.[3] Some of these changes came slowly. Women did not receive the vote in either France or Italy until 1944 and 1945, respectively, and in England the vote was restricted to women over 30. In France married women remained legal minors until 1938. Meanwhile, the war did propel some working-class women socially and economically upward into the burgeoning service sector, where they found economic independence and stability. They could also mingle with middle-class women, many of whom had to support themselves or supplement family incomes following the wartime demise of bourgeois business fortunes.

Still, in the interwar years women of all classes were generally segregated into low-paying, low-prestige jobs, shut out of lucrative and influential management positions as corporations merged, and forced out of their wartime jobs through a variety of government policies designed to provide employment for demobilized soldiers. Although there was no significant increase in the number of working women in the United States until World War II, the Great War facilitated two shifts in employment patterns: white women replaced white men in heavy industry, transportation, and offices, and black women replaced some black men and white women in low-paying, backbreaking, unskilled labor. In nations other than the United States, most of the social welfare provisions that had been offered during the war—child care in particular—were later eliminated in the interest of "repopulating" countries now depleted of young men. In other words, women's emergence into the public world of employment proved a temporary hiatus from their "natural" task of child-rearing.

The "New" New Woman

But most important for our purposes, after the war female sexuality became the symbolic center of social anarchy and moral deviance. Of course, the fin de siècle had marked the beginning of a period of antifeminist backlash as new legislation sought to regulate sexual expression and female sexuality in particular. In Progressive Era America, commentators had already remarked on the increasing "sexualization" of society—William Marion Moody, the editor of the *St. Louis Mirror*, declared in 1910 that it was "Sex O'Clock in America."[4]

Yet the interwar years provided a fresh focus for anxiety about changing social order: another "new woman." This new woman was quite different from her suffragist predecessors. She was generally not a feminist, partly because warmongers, and even many women's suffrage activists, declared the fight for women's rights unpatriotic. She was doggedly heterosexual, partly because sexologists, who became popular during the interwar years, stigmatized not only lesbian relationships but all female friendship, which they believed posed the risk of lesbianism. As Carroll Smith-Rosenberg has argued, "The daughter's quest for heterosexual pleasures, not the mother's demand for political power, now personified female freedom" (283). For those determined to preserve traditional gender and class divisions, the new woman (I will continue to refer to her this way) became a source of anxiety, for she was a "public" woman—she worked—and she expected sexual fulfillment, or at least the pleasure of nonprocreative sexual encounters. That is, she was a public woman but she was not a prostitute, and worse yet, she often came from the middle class.

The Frenchman Victor Margueritte's infamous 1922 novel about the "new" woman, *La Garçonne* (The Bachelor Girl), sold over a million copies, was translated into 12 languages, and earned its author expulsion from the Legion of Honor. As Mary Louise Roberts has argued, it alarmed cultural critics not just because it depicts a sexually promiscuous woman who sleeps with both women and men, bobs her hair, goes to bars, and smokes, but because its heroine is a white middle-class girl from a respectable family.[5] During the interwar years the distinction between "good" and "bad" women became increasingly blurred as young, middle-class, single women cut their hair, donned comfortable clothes, drove, worked, had male companions, played sports, and earned names such as *garçonne* and flapper. It was as if all women had taken on the attributes of prostitutes or lesbians, as many commentators indeed suggested.[6] Maurice Hamel complained that prostitution was "everywhere," a "torrent" in which modern society was being "submerged" (quoted in Dean 1992, 70). As Louis Martin-Chauffier put it in his response to a 1926 survey of views about homosexuality: "We are surrounded by inverts and these inverts no longer hide themselves." Most of the other respondents echoed this view about both female and male "inverts."[7]

Although most cultural critics bemoaned the loss of moral standards among men and women alike, the metaphor for social anarchy was above all the sexually promiscuous woman, who destabilized the boundaries between genders and classes. Atina Grossman has suggested that in Germany men complained of not being able to tell the difference between "honest women and whores."[8] In America, Eleanor Wembridge, a critic of college student mores, noted that "the sex manners of uncultivated and uncritical people have become the manners for all" (quoted in White, 167). As American "middle-class women became more sexually available, men began to speak of them in ways they previously talked only of working-class women or prostitutes" (165). The new explicitness of female sexual desire challenged Victorian gender ideology and class structure by openly opposing the female sexual repression on which they were based. In choosing her partners and acting on her desires, the new woman was perceived as no different from a man. The following analysis explores how the new woman's sexual "promiscuity" expressed the loss of the natural foundations of sexual difference.

The New Woman and Mass Culture

After the Great War the regimentation associated with daily work routines expanded. Although urbanization and industrialization were hardly new phenomena, the automation of factories nearly transposed men and women into robots. Following the principles of "Taylorism" (after the American efficiency engineer Frederick Taylor), assembly lines were built to use human bodies as if they were efficient machines. The introduction of cars and new visual media (such as cinema), as well as the increased accessibility of ready-made clothes and other consumer items (such as vacuum cleaners and washing machines), effected a social reorganization of the senses. Male commentators conceived these phenomena as part of a process of "rationalization," as it was called in Germany; perceptions of women's bodies expressed their impact further. In particular, the regimented sensuality of the cancan and the British Tiller Girls, dubbed "mass ornament entertainment" by the critic Siegfried Kracauer, mirrored the rationality of production lines: "When they tapped their feet in fast tempo, it sounded like *business, business*; when they kicked their legs with mathematic precision, they joyously affirmed the progress of rationalization."[9]

The film critic Patrice Petro, returning to the earliest critiques of mass culture in Weimar Germany, has argued that critics expressed ambivalence toward the effects of mass culture through the "metaphorical figure of the woman," which "stands as much for modernity as it does for the continually renewed search for a lost plenitude" (135). In such critiques—Petro is thinking of Siegfried Kracauer's, Walter Benjamin's, and Theodor Adorno's—mass culture entertainment replicates the rationalized modern world and thus participates in this complex reorganization of sense perception. In Petro's account, women become allegories of the quintessential expression of modernity and mass culture: the city. Woman is as tantalizing, alluring, and demonic as the visual pleasure of cinema, city lights, and cabarets. She is thus seductive and dangerous. At the same time woman, like the streamlined, time-conscious crowd in the city, is rationalized and remote—Kracauer's assembly-line entertainment, for example, or the indifferent gestures of the new woman. Woman is seductive and illusory (like the movies), anonymous and easy to lose in urban crowds, but she is also an open book, on display, her movements as predictable as those of well-oiled machinery.[10]

The War Veteran and the New Woman

Women's bodies thus became allegories for mass culture and the dehumanizing effects of modernity. Moreover, "new" women became the most visible symbol of a general emasculation (and hence dehumanization) effected by the war. By all contemporary accounts, the war emasculated men and permitted women to take their place. The new "civilization without sexes," as the French writer and war veteran Drieu la Rochelle put it, represented the dehumanization of a civilization that prided itself on its humanistic, liberal virtues.[11]

In this general interpretation, the war quite literally turned men into cannon fodder in the interests of the nation, as fighting with sophisticated weaponry marked the end of hand-to-hand combat and the beginning of wars with faceless enemies. The battle, understood historically as a proving ground of manhood, had become a rationalized, dehumanized process in which men sat in miles of trenches up to their necks in water with dead comrades and rats and passively awaited gunfire from an enemy they could not see. Meanwhile, government propaganda denied this loss of manhood and encouraged the belief at home that the war was noble, heroic, and manly. Paul Fussell's famous example of the mock trench set up by the British government in Kensington Gardens makes this disjunction explicit: in the exhibit their sisters, wives, and lovers went to see, soldiers were depicted drinking tea comfortably in the dug-out earth—a far cry from the reality of the war.[12]

Scholars have argued that men displaced this feeling of alienation from the homefront—their sense of impotence and resentment at being reduced to instruments of a war machine and depleted of individuality—onto women. Susan Kingsley Kent has recently noted that the Great War was often represented as an extension of the "sex war" between men and women.[13] Through a sustained analysis of interwar French novels, one historian argues that the behavior attributed to the sexually promiscuous woman in fact mirrors the experience of the war veteran (Roberts, 56–62). When the soldier returns home from battle, he is unable to sustain personal relationships; he is literally or figuratively impotent and hence sterile, like the nonprocreative woman. The senseless violence of the war produced a man lacking in moral self-restraint who himself committed senseless acts of violence (usually against women), indulged in drink to excess, and refused human connection and commitment. Klaus Theweleit's famous studies of German "male fantasies"—soldiers' visceral repudiation of fluidity, fusion, and femininity in favor of phallic hardness and well-defined boundaries—also suggest the veteran's projections of his feelings of helplessness onto femininity and women.[14]

The literature of this period demonstrates the same sort of displacement. Misogyny and fear of femininity were already evident in fin-de-siècle novels that equated female sexuality with dangerous contagion, contaminated blood, and loss of boundaries—Bram Stoker's *Dracula* and Émile Zola's *Nana*, for example. Now novels grappled explicitly with the new woman, from best-sellers like Margueritte's *La Garçonne* and Marcel Prévost's *Les Don Juanes* to high-culture texts by D. H. Lawrence, Ernest Hemingway, and T. S. Eliot. The French commentator Jean Cassou complained that the garçonne led to a "lowering of literary standards," and another critic, Henriette Charasson, asserted that she "impoverished" literature and rendered it "languid" and "impotent"; neither critic explained how or why (quoted in *Les Marges*, 28, 27).

The New Woman and the City

As the delineation between masculinity and femininity became ever more tenuous, femininity ceased to function as a stable referent against which masculinity could define itself. Certain interwar writings on women and the city make this development very clear. Recounting in his journal his time in Berlin, the Englishman Harold Nicholson allegorized modern European cities as women in different phases of life. He seeks to ferret out the sexual secrets beneath the surfaces of the morally reputable exteriors of cities like London, Paris, and Berlin. "London is an old lady in black lace and diamonds who guards her secrets with dignity." Paris, he continues, is "a woman in the prime of life to whom one would only tell those secrets which one desires not to be repeated." But Berlin "is a girl in a pullover, not much powder on her face, Hölderlin in her pocket . . . a heart which is almost too ready to sympathize, and a breadth of view which charms one's repressions" (quoted in Petro, 116).

Some of the connections Nicholson draws between female figures and cities are rather conventional—London as the repressed if dignified puritanical lady, Paris as the discreet and mature woman in whom everyone confides.[15] But Berlin is no conventional woman: she is the new woman who dresses casually, wears little makeup, and has intellectual pretensions. Unlike her suffragist forebears, as

I noted earlier, she tends to be apolitical and a devout heterosexual. Nevertheless, she represents a "maximum irritant for the nerves" (116) because she oscillates between masculine pretensions and feminine naïveté. At the same time she has a big heart, and her intellect is not sophisticated but "charming"—frivolous, unthreatening, and ultimately relaxing. Finally, then, this "maximum irritant" is "corrected by a maximum sedative" (116).

Berlin evokes an ambivalent response at best, both irritating and charming, both masculine and feminine. To Nicholson's weary senses, Berlin represents the blurring of gender difference. On the one hand, Berlin is stripped of sexuality and hence stripped of secrets. On the other hand, Berlin is feminized and is thus alluring, "charming." That city is both utterly "irritating"—without sexuality and the secrets sexuality entails—and sedating. Although Nicholson makes clear how femininity is linked to secrecy in his characterizations of London and Paris, he is not at all clear about what sexual secrets Berlin reveals or will not reveal. Rather, Berlin represents a secret that will never be betrayed, a mystery that will never be solved, and that mystery reflects Nicholson's own inability to define femininity in clear terms. The city's authentically warm and sedative effects are so inextricable from its irritating, pretentious, and inauthentic ones that conventional femininity has been lost—at least by modern Berlin.

The German writer Carl Zuckmayer also mourned the loss of conventional femininity when he described Berlin as the woman of one's desires. "To conquer Berlin was to conquer the world. The only thing was . . . that you had to take all the hurdles again and again, had to break through the goal again and again in order to maintain your position" (quoted in Petro, 117). The "new" woman becomes the allegory of this endless series of hurdles. Men want to conquer Berlin, tempted by the seductive allure of a woman who is both "hefty" and "full-breasted" and a "mere wisp of a thing, with boyish legs in black silk stockings" (117). That is, her posturing as both masculine and feminine constitutes a secret that men want to reveal or "conquer" and never can.

Other commentators mourned the loss of femininity still more explicitly. Reflecting on the *garçonne* of the 1920s, the Frenchman Pierre Lièvre moaned that a woman with short hair has lost her mystery: "One well knows that she can no longer transform herself in the bedroom: one knows her exactly as she is" (quoted in Roberts, 75). The illusion Lièvre demanded accompanied one of women's supposedly natural functions—to please men. This illusion did not cross the line between private and public, or between masculinity and femininity, but rather confirmed it. Women's performance was coterminous with the social role ascribed to her gender; her performance, always private, at once deluded her audience and revealed her authentic or true femininity: the desire to please and nurture others. The seductive, illusion-creating powers traditionally attributed to women can be neutralized only if a man thinks he knows what is underneath a woman's machinations. In that case, he simply plays a game of courtship in which the woman takes on the delightful role of adorning and covering herself (of performing) for his benefit.

The French feminist lawyer Maria Verone, defending the new woman, argued, in contrast to Lièvre, that now men could see women "as they are," since their naturalness, short hair, and unconstrained clothing precluded the duplicity that previously led to "false sentiments" and "loveless marriages" (quoted in Roberts, 81). Verone sought to assure men like Lièvre that women were still women. In the tradition of French feminism since the eighteenth century, she sought to counter negative images of femininity: if women were permitted to be men's equals, they would command more respect and make better, more authentic, and presumably more "feminine" companions. They would not (as Mary Wollstonecraft and Marie-Olympe de Gouges had already argued in defense of women's rights a century before) be forced to play politics from the sidelines and hence to use manipulative tactics to influence powerful men. By rendering women pure, honest, and transparent, independence would paradoxically reinforce the boundary between public and private.

Regardless of Verone's assertions, it was no longer clear to everyone just what a woman was. Was she most herself when wrapped in a mysterious aura or when stripped of it? The new, less constrained fashions worn by Verone and other new women reinforced that confusion, regardless of how they chose to justify their bobbed hair. As much as Verone emphasized the naturalness, and therefore the "true" femininity, of the female body, it was impossible to extricate such naturalness from masculine posturing. However "feminine" women assumed themselves to be, when they postured as men's equals or imitators (as indicated by the comments of Nicholson, Zuckmayer, and Lièvre), they called into question the naturalness— the proper place and different constitution—of femininity itself.

Thus, to come full circle, when Berl attributed the loss of self to urban anomie, he described a world of tensions very different from the urban anxieties of the Victorian age. In the Victorian vision of modern life, the private sphere had compensated for public isolation and alienation, and middle-class women's virtue had stood for all that was good and true. In Berl's world, by contrast, the boundaries between masculine and feminine, public and private, and the middle and working classes were not differentiated. Berl described a world in which the distinctly gendered self was no longer distinct— chiefly because femininity could no longer be located, pinned down, or regulated as it once had been.

Interwar Homosexuality

This period's uncertainty about gender boundaries was again most dramatically represented by images of homosexuality, and of female homosexuality in particular.[16] Cultural critics and legislators were as obsessed with this subject as nineteenth-century men had been. Literary critics observed a transition from a "literature of homosexuals" to a "homosexual literature," thus reconceiving contained identities as contagious ones that had infiltrated all of contemporary literature (quoted in *Les Marges*, 57). Many commentators were incensed by André Gide's 1924 *Corydon*, in which, following the tradition established by *Der Eigene*, he defended male homosexuality by referring to its practice in ancient Greece. A Dr. François Nazier wrote that *Corydon* "was only the manifestation, astonishing, it is true, of the strange proselytizing furor which now inhabits the apostles of homosexuality [*l'amour à l'envers*] as it does a delirious saint."[17] The first parts of Marcel Proust's less lofty portrait of homosexuality, translated into English as *The Cities of the Plain*, also appeared in 1921.

Writers and politicians everywhere believed inversion was on the rise. It refused to hide itself, and they decried the putatively emasculating effects of its visibility. In the United States the psychiatrist Edward Kemp invented the "homosexual panic disorder" in 1920 to describe the latent homosexuality he discovered in his work with war veterans who had been in gender-segregated environments for prolonged periods. His diagnostic label made homosexuality visible even among men who were profoundly committed to denying such "perverse sexual cravings."[18] This anxiety extended to the new woman, who, as the critic Gerard Bauer noted, sometimes consciously but mostly unconsciously imitated homosexual men: like homosexual men, he said, the *garçonne* was sexually promiscuous and afraid of "real men" (quoted in *Les Marges*, 24).

Thus, critics used the analogy of homosexual men to assert that the garçonne's apparent virility was merely a pretense—an admission of the desire for a real masculinity she could never possess. In contrast, the lesbianism of which she was often accused marked her as ambivalent, rather than as "lacking" virility. Although Radclyffe Hall's lesbian novel *The Well of Loneliness*, judged obscene in 1928, helped to popularize pejorative images of the "mannish lesbian"—sexually aggressive, atavistic, and sterile—other less predictable images also emerged during this period. Margaret Roellig, the author of a book on *The Lesbians of Berlin*, alluded to their virility, but she no longer opposed that virility to hyperfemininity. She abandoned the incoherent fin-de-siècle effort to make lesbian sexuality conform to gender norms by insisting lesbians' "virility" was compatible with female sexuality. Roellig discarded all notions of inversion-vice in favor of a less tortured and convoluted but no less paradoxical construction of lesbianism. The problem was no longer how to distinguish congenital lesbianism from acquired lesbianism, but how to represent lesbians' virility without conflating it with masculinity. As Roellig describes them, these "men-women" are supple and graceful; they have good taste and good looks and count many distinguished women among their number. Their virility is sensual and distinct from masculinity, although it is masculine.[19]

In short, lesbianism was again destroying the line of demarcation between the genders: it did not represent a complete or incomplete sexual identity but marked the fluidity of gender boundaries. Perhaps because of this function, it was also depicted as contagious. Lesbians were outlaws or "creatures of the night"; they lived both in broad daylight and "in the shadows" (Roellig, 50). In the nineteenth century the problem was to ferret out those who looked like everyone else but in fact lived in the shadows. By the interwar years shadow and light had become indistinguishable as the new woman marked the porous border between masculinity and femininity and between homosexuality and heterosexuality.

For both the Left and Right, the new woman's sexuality became the ultimate commodity, the symbol of a world in which meaning and connection were fleeting and transient, and illusion could no longer be differentiated from reality. Women's sexual assertiveness confirmed conservatives' worst fears that popular culture was dangerous because it distracted citizens from the productive, orderly, and regulated pleasures of civilized society. But the new woman also confirmed radicals' fears that the "masses" would fall under the spell of seductive pleasures and lose their capacity for resistance to the false gratification promised by capitalist commodities.

The more cultural critics, legislators, and other authorities tried to reaffirm gender boundaries during the interwar years, the more the "new" woman's sexuality marked such boundaries as illusory. Masculinity and femininity had become nothing but images dependent on each other for their own cultural meaning. The gendered self had to be continually renewed, for it was nothing but an illusion, an image with no depth or clear referent.

4

The Sexual Revolution

> There is too much fathering going on now and there is no doubt about it fathers are depressing.
>
> —Gertrude Stein, *Everybody's Autobiography* (1937)

After the war, men's reclaiming of selfhood was inseparable from the need to redefine gender difference in new terms—terms that could no longer rely on natural distinctions between masculinity and femininity (or between gender and sexuality). Yet throughout the 1920s and 1930s legislators, cultural critics, politicians, and war veterans sought to restore normative gender roles at a moment when women were most vehemently asserting their "right" to sexual pleasure.

The so-called roaring twenties are famous for their liberalization of attitudes toward sexuality, including female sexuality. But as historians such as Nancy Cott and Linda Gordon have persuasively argued, the 1920s and 1930s were also a period of backlash, under the guise of liberation, against women's rights and feminism more generally.[1] Françoise Thébaud writes that "the stereotypes of the flapper and the liberated female were more often invoked to denounce the collapse of the sex barrier and the double standard than to applaud the victories of the women's movement" (2). I have already discussed the broader context of this backlash. I now hope to demonstrate that our understanding of the relationship between sexuality and the self originates here, in the ambivalence of the interwar period.

Scientific Management and the Sexual Revolution

Almost all social policies created during the interwar years and since then have been efforts to address a perceived decline in heterosexual, familial responsibility—both men's and women's inability to be monogamous, their desire to remain childless, and their glorification of personal freedom. These policies differed, however, from the prewar social purist campaigns, which called for repressive legislation against prostitution, pornography, and all "deviant" forms of sexual expression.

Social purists sought to persuade the state to repress forms of sexual expression that threatened gender, race, and class boundaries. They were often allied with so-called hygiene movements (the American Social Hygiene Association, the French National League for Mental Hygiene, and so forth), as well as with eugenicists and neo-Malthusians (after the population theorist Thomas Malthus), who had long advocated government prevention programs to educate the population so as to improve its "quality." These different movements overlapped in their aims. Neo-Malthusians believed that population control would best be achieved by legalizing contraception. Among their ranks were those concerned with racial degeneration as well as feminists promoting women's freedom from child-rearing. In England they founded a group as early as the 1870s and later counted among their members George Bernard Shaw and others involved in the reform-minded Fabian society. In France, Paul Robin founded the Neo-Malthusian League in 1896. In 1905 the middle-class German feminist Helene Stöcker established the League for the Protection of Maternity and Sexual Reform, which advocated free access to contraception; in 1911 she founded the Committee for Birth Control to disseminate contraceptive information. Thus, for the first time birth control (a term invented by the American feminist Margaret Sanger) was no longer the informal practice it had been for centuries but a formal technology.

Eugenicists, after Francis Galton, applied Mendelian laws of inheritance to human populations. They were often considered too radical by other groups because their most fanatical members advocated extreme infringements on personal liberty. However, neo-Malthusians and members of hygiene movements who pursued improvements in public health through state intervention were also motivated by the desire to improve racial "purity" and hence regulate populations in the interest of the state. Mobilized by the fear of "racial degeneration" and low birth rates, eugenicists, Neo-Malthusians and social hygiene advocates all sought in different ways, in different countries, and with varying degrees of success, not to repress information about sexuality and birth control but to disseminate it. In the United States and Scandinavian countries, for example, eugenics was very successful early on: between 1907 and 1913, 12 states introduced eugenic sterilization (mostly of male criminals) and marriage prohibitions, and in the 1920s and 1930s sterilization legislation was passed in Denmark, Norway, Sweden, Iceland, and Germany. In France, eugenics had a small if significant following.[2]

The war gave new impetus and legitimacy to these movements, both because it justified increased state intervention in the private sphere—in health, family welfare, and so forth—and because it exacerbated the sense of moral crisis. Furthermore, the scientific approach to moral problems had been increasingly legitimated as repressive solutions failed, the medical profession increased its power, and socialists manipulated scientific language to encourage state intervention to improve working-class conditions. The neutral language of science was more acceptable to twentieth-century sensibilities than the moralizing tone of the social purity movements, and it helped win the approval of the European and North American public.

In England, for example, more working-class women than men supported eugenics because they believed sterilization might curb the male "sex drive," thus decreasing the number of children they were forced to bear and reducing instances of sexual assault.[3] German socialists advocated contraception because they believed it was cruel to encourage childbirth in economically deprived families.[4]

During the interwar years sexology became institutionalized. In 1919 Magnus Hirschfeld established an institutional home for the sexological movement in Berlin, the Institute for Sexual Science, whose funding and management he ceded to the government in 1924. A series of "International Congresses for Sex Reform" were held in Berlin (1921), Copenhagen (1928), London (1929), Vienna (1930), and Brno, Czechoslovakia (1932). In 1923 a professorship of racial hygiene was funded at Munich University, and in 1927 the

Kaiser Wilhelm Society established the Kaiser Wilhelm Institute for Anthropology, Human Heredity, and Eugenics, also in Berlin. Its financial support came from both the Reich and Prussia. In England and the United States, figures such as Havelock Ellis, Edward Carpenter, Ellen Key (a Swede by birth), and the formidable Englishwoman Marie Stopes—whose *Married Love* was published, with the help of the Malthusian League, in 1920—couched their promotion of birth control, eugenics, and sexual liberation, especially for women, in a matter-of-fact approach to sexuality that rapidly gained acceptance.

The new attitudes toward sexuality represented an important shift away from Victorian mores. Although married heterosexuality continued to be privileged, individual male and female sexual expression was increasingly celebrated as well. In radical Greenwich Village circles, sexuality represented authentic self-expression in an inauthentic, repressive Victorian culture. A vibrant intellectual and bohemian culture also thrived in Harlem. Although its clubs served as a refuge for both black and white sexual dissidents, they also attracted many middle-class, heterosexual whites who sought an escape from the puritanical culture they perceived in conventional white society. Harlem gave these fugitives from white society a chance to indulge in an exotic, primitivist fantasy about black culture and the sexuality of African Americans. In Nella Larsen's 1929 novella *Passing*, a black woman explains to a white man why white women frequent Harlem dances: "I think what they feel is—well, a kind of emotional excitement. You know, the sort of thing you feel in the presence of something strange, and even, perhaps, a bit repugnant to you."[5]

Outside bohemian circles, sexuality was still conceived—as social purists believed it should be—within the confines of a profound, marital, spiritual union. Nevertheless, the emphasis on procreation shifted to an emphasis on pleasure, and the emphasis on men's sexual needs began to accommodate a recognition of women's sexual desire. Sexual pleasure was now privileged as perhaps the most important component of a healthy marriage. Men were instructed to attend carefully to their wives' sexual needs, and an entire industry of sex manuals and advice literature taught them how.

While this advice literature was couched in clinical terms—often to get past the censors—its purpose was ultimately to help couples achieve "true" spiritual union in the materialistic modern world. Through clear, physiological description, Marie Stopes sought to help married couples enjoy a fulfilling sex life in order to enhance their spiritual well-being. Her book *Married Love* argues that sexual ignorance interferes with true love: "Every heart desires a mate . . . neither man nor woman singly can know the joy of the performance of all the human functions; neither man nor woman singly can create another human-being . . . and there is nothing for which the innermost spirit of one and all so yearns as for a sense of union with another soul, and the perfecting of oneself which such union brings."[6]

Stopes combined sexual information with allusions to romance, tied sexuality to marriage, and condemned abortion. This mixture shielded her work from the censors. Her respectability also helped her to gain the support of the medical profession, which had been active in Malthusian and eugenic movements and sought to increase its power. Stopes was as influential as the Dutch gynecologist Theodoor Hendrik Van De Velde, whose *Marriage: Its Physiology and Technique* (1926) expresses the same attitudes and sold widely in Germany, England, and the United States.[7]

The Welfare State and Sexual Equality

It is necessary to understand that this new attitude and vocabulary used by Stopes and others continued to repress and regulate sexuality. For what purposes? How, in particular, was it employed and manipulated by the state? Professionals and politicians paradoxically conceived state intervention as a means of securing the boundaries between the public and private spheres that had been blurred by the Great War. They defined the family and monogamous heterosexual love as an emotional fortress, which they proposed to guard against attack by making new kinds of intervention in family life. In contrast to late nineteenth–century social purity movements, they sought not to repress sexual expression but to regulate it through educational and other measures designed to prevent deviance before it occurred. They believed that ignoring modern mores would be counterproductive; only by acknowledging that the boundaries between private and public spheres, and hence gender roles, had been compromised by the war could those boundaries begin to be reconstituted. In short, they believed that using overtly repressive measures to cope with moral crisis would only create alluring taboos.

Of course, the shift from moral to scientific language, and hence from one kind of repressive discourse about sexuality to an apparently more liberal but equally regulatory one, met with resistance in many circles. Still, it was supported by both the Left and the Right, for both camps championed new, technocratic forms of social organization to scientifically manage populations, whether to improve their "quality" or their standard of living. The matter-of-factness and neutrality of scientific discourse—its apparent lack of a moral agenda—contributed to its triumph and endurance, even to the present day (I am thinking, for example, of the popular work of Masters and Johnson). Thus, the new openness with which sexuality was discussed was inseparable from the state's efforts—and unprecedented license—to control populations in new and more effective ways.

Historians have discussed this shift from moral to scientific solutions to social problems primarily by analyzing social movements or the development of the welfare state. More recently, feminist historians have criticized the presumption that these movements and the welfare state served to control populations without reference to gender. Since the private and public spheres are themselves gendered, the state's paradoxical interwar effort to resolidify the boundary between them must have had different implications for male and female sexuality. In fact, that effort cannot be understood without accounting for the way the public regulation of sexuality was specifically aimed at controlling women's sexuality—or at controlling the heterosexual, middle and working-class couple by controlling women's sexuality.

In most countries the democratic welfare state sustained the gendered division of labor—in order to raise the number of healthy births—by helping women reconcile the demands of child-rearing and work. The German government encouraged poor women to have children through protectionist legislation that offered subsidies to mothers. Feminist demands that the state recognize child-rearing as unpaid labor converged with democratic regimes' concerns about decreased population, especially after the war. Thus, the atmosphere of greater tolerance toward women's sexuality, expressed primarily through some liberalization of contraception, was also marked by hostility to full reproductive rights and by staunchly pronatalist regulation. Even the more liberal attitudes toward contraception can easily be interpreted as allowing working-class women to space births, making child-rearing economically feasible and less cumbersome. That is, by improving working-class conditions, politicians on the Left believed they would also increase population by lowering the mortality rate.

In Weimar Germany increased protection for motherhood and more lenient attitudes toward contraception were coupled with the continued regulation of abortion. In 1927 the government granted extended maternity leave and protected pregnant women and working mothers from dismissal. That same year, after several decades of using paragraph 184 of the penal code to suppress literature about contraception, the government legalized "inoffensive" contraceptive propaganda. Abortion, however, remained a criminal offense.

The sex reform movement in Weimar Germany was dominated by doctors who wanted to ease the sufferings of working-class people and working-class women in particular. Like Stopes, these reform advocates also sought to defend the traditional family and hence support heterosexual, married unions. As Atina Grossmann has written, "The Weimar Sex Reform movement . . . presents to us a 'sexual revolution' in all its complexity and ambiguity: sexual satisfaction for women, but satisfaction proclaimed and defined mainly by men; the right to contraception and abortion, but only when 'necessary'; active sexuality justified because it was healthy and potentially procreative; orgasm as a eugenic measure" (155).

In the United States Margaret Sanger founded the American Birth Control League in 1921, but contraception remained illegal; not until 1936 would the Supreme Court remove birth control devices from prosecution under antiobscenity law. The following year the American Medical Association approved the dispensing of contraceptives by doctors, a measure that primarily helped white, middle-class women who enjoyed regular medical care. Many physicians nevertheless remained hostile to birth control because they believed it contributed to social and moral degeneration: they insisted, as many moralists do today, that contraception permitted and even encouraged otherwise virtuous girls to indulge in sexual pleasure because they would no longer fear conception.

Sanger spent time in England to avoid prosecution under American laws, but she was not spared there either. Her pamphlet on *Family Limitation* was prosecuted as obscene, and two Communists, Guy Aldred and his wife Rose Witcop, were prosecuted in 1923 for selling it. Marie Stopes, however, continued to find fertile soil in Britain for her enterprises. In 1921 she founded the Society for Constructive Birth Control and Racial Progress and adopted

Sanger's principles for the society: its goals were to stabilize populations, prevent abortion, and promote marital harmony. Stopes had already opened one family planning clinic in 1918, and by 1939 two-thirds of such clinics operated with the aid of state funds. In 1930 the Labour-controlled health ministry lifted the ban preventing maternity and child welfare centers from offering advice on contraception. The British Medical Association and the Anglican Church also sanctioned birth control if the mother's health depended on it, and after 1938 abortion could be performed to relieve a mother's physical or emotional distress.

Women's rights activists and socialists thus achieved far less than total victory. In France, the democratic country most dramatically plagued by demographic concerns, legislators passed a uniquely draconian antiabortion law in 1920 and revised it in equally severe terms in 1923: it forbade even the advocacy of birth control or abortion and imposed fines ranging from 100 to 3,000 francs on so-called perpetrators. In addition, it imposed prison sentences from six months to three years on abortion patients and the doctors who helped them. Fascist governments—particularly Italy after 1922 and Germany after 1933—simply banned all reproductive rights and paid state subsidies to fathers rather than mothers. (In Germany, the ban applied only to women deemed racially "pure.")[8]

In spite of popular images and the intentions of its advocates, the sexual revolution did not liberate women's sexuality: it was a revolution on men's terms. In other words, the sexual revolution was predicated on the interests of patriarchal heterosexuality, with which many women concurred.

Most historians thus describe the shift in sexual mores as a new and more effective means of population control, in the interests of the ruling class, or as a new means of controlling challenges to conventional gender divisions. Some socialist feminist historians link these arguments by theorizing about class, gender, and race simultaneously and by stressing the important role women's groups have played in raising the status of mothers' labor. The feminist model of social control provides a persuasive and powerful means of understanding how an apparently liberatory movement effected both social transformation and social control. Feminist historians have revealed that sexual revolutionaries often expressed equality, paradoxically, in terms of gender difference. Marie Stopes, Havelock Ellis, and even the Greenwich Village bohemians insisted that satisfying heterosexual relationships could be achieved only by equalizing desire, not its forms of expression or its purposes. Most, though not all, condemned nonheterosexual and adulterous liaisons and linked women's sexual desire to increased procreation. In short, the sexual revolution did not grant women sexual equality.

But it did redefine sexual equality. In their response to the threats posed by democratization, elite men did not simply try to conserve gender ideology—they transformed it. Legislators, politicians, cultural critics, war veterans, and others sought to restore compromised manhood, to restore an integrated, authentically masculine, and above all "natural" self. Sexual equality no longer referred to the liberation of desires traditionally associated with prostitutes, homosexuals, and now women more generally, but, as I will argue, to the restoration of an expressive, distinctly male self that had been commodified and reified by pornography, by consumerism, and especially by war.

Male Sexuality, De-repression, and Discipline

Across great professional and political divides, elite men reconstituted sexuality as beautiful, for it represented corporeal wholeness. Already in 1914 Havelock Ellis had claimed that the "task" of "social hygiene" was to teach young men how to respect rather than despise the body. He insisted that only through sex education could they be taught a proper "reverence for the body," and that frank talk about adulterous, homosexual, and other longings would "help to steady the individual and prove a check against disrespect to his body."[9] Ellis thus equated the achievement of monogamous, heterosexual, reproductive—that is to say, "healthy"—sexuality with a (phantasmic) corporeal integrity that guaranteed psychological as well as social stability. He endorsed rational sexual education rather than censorship as the most effective means of combating perversion; taboos only made the forbidden more desirable. He held that pornography, for example, would hold no temptation for the well-educated mind. "Secrecy and repression," he argued, are "against nature" (1914, 124, 137).

The general discourse about sexuality's healthiness found expression in D. H. Lawrence's recommendation that individuals "practice facing up to their sexuality and achieving its . . . sublimation."[10] Referring specifically to "aesthetic" sublimation, Lawrence sought to channel sexuality into the making of great literature; he thought pornography was emasculating and "dirty." Most other narratives sought to free sexuality—to "face up to it"—in order to channel it into some useful or higher purpose and to neutralize its formidable and hence socially and psychically disruptive power.

Facing up to their sexuality enabled men to protect the purity and integrity of their bodies against various forms of psychic, social, and corporeal dissolution, such as impotence, sterility, and meaningless violence. Medical men, psychologists, and others now conceived perversion as the *consequence* of censorship and other less formal means of sexual regulation; like Ellis, they believed honest discussion about sexuality guaranteed the triumph of "nature" over perversion. The prominent American psychologist Granville Stanley Hall, the founder of American child psychology, expressed similar views on the consequences of repression.[11] One French commentator on the Left, Lionel d'Autrec, noted that the same politicians who permitted detailed descriptions of murder and glorified war suppressed the "most normal and most beautiful of all human acts."[12] The same men who denounced moral laxity "die while being caressed by a prostitute . . . die in the arms of a pederast" (92). "All the democracy's elite," he declared, "take opium and have themselves flagellated in the houses on the rue Miromesnil" (287).

The Restoration of Virility

Antiwar commentators contrasted these images of a debauched "democracy's elite" with the self-sacrifice of the soldiers who fought at the front. Politicians' betrayal of the nation's youth was expressed in terms of a contrast between old men's unhealthy, repressed, hypocritical sexuality and the vigorous sexual instincts of young men slain for no purpose. In the diverse works of this period, prostitutes symbolized the illusion to which the elderly men who constituted democracy's elites succumbed. Interwar images of prostitution thus rendered (unregulated) female sexuality oddly complicit with the war and hence with mass murder.

Like war, the prostitute offered a seductive, virility-enhancing conquest, a "territory" to conquer. Yet she was also a soul-destroying, profit-making, virility-stripping machine. She was the "grand illusion" to which men succumbed at their peril; her facade dissipated quickly, with bloody consequences. She promised self-possession and ensured self-loss.

Again and again, this image of the prostitute was compared to that of the new woman, whose promiscuity, aggression, and allure seemed equally treacherous. How, men asked, could they be expected to tell the difference between call girls and pure girls, between prostitutes and "new women"? The interwar assault on prostitution thus replicated earlier appraisals of the new woman, rendering her a figure of men's ambivalence toward the war and toward modernity more generally.

After the war democrats and fascists alike sought above all a means of differentiating "honest" women from the dishonest ones who were all too ready to "stab you in the back." The phrase was popular with those Germans who felt that the Weimar government had betrayed the national interest (by signing the Versailles Treaty), and it quite literally described the feelings of many war veterans who returned home to find themselves betrayed by a wife or lover. The quest for transparency, for a world in which men said what they meant and meant what they said—the desire never to be taken by surprise—took shape through the reconstruction of sexuality as a virile, masculine, and purifying force.

Many critics claimed that in the name of restoring virility, politicians undermined it and turned soldiers into passive and hence feminized instruments of a war machine. The French legal scholar Paul Lapeire similarly noted that in regulating men's "genital activity" the state robbed them of their individuality and hence of their virility—so that, for example, censorship laws did not preserve the nation from emasculation, as legislators had hoped, but instead encouraged it. After the Great War, Lapeire and others demonized the forces of repression for constraining the instincts that made "nations and races" great. Repression no longer acted as a constraint that guaranteed the freedom of all by balancing individual and social needs—the necessary task of the liberal state—but sapped morale and reduced man to nothing other than a "lowly cog" in a "gigantic machine . . . less and less free to do what he will with his activity and his body."[13] The repression of sexuality in the form of obscenity law was only a surreptitious means by which politicians emasculated young men while feeding them delusions of virility. In short, repression encouraged rather than inhibited moral degeneration.

The purpose of sexual openness, in this view, would be not to "free" sexuality so that everyone could act according to his or her desires, but to face up to desire so that it might be more effectively regulated. This rather paradoxical insistence that the de-repression of sexuality would lead to the end of immorality was not about freeing sexual instincts but about helping men to remain men. Understood in this way, de-repression was not equated with the dissolution of corporeal boundaries, the loss of discipline and hence the acting out of dangerous longings. Instead, de-repressed sexuality was redefined as continuous with the phallic, boundaried, and hence masculine self war veterans strove to recover. In other words, sexual expression was now reconciled with, rather than opposed to, the restraint and self-mastery that defined the ideal citizen.

The Reconciliation of Sexuality and The Self

In reconciling sexual expression with self-restraint, cultural critics reconstructed the relationship between masculinity and moral order. Although censorship laws were not seriously modified until the 1960s (see chapter 5), their advocates began to change their attitudes toward the obscene by making a distinction between erotic, healthy, masculine literature and "vulgar" pornography. Masculinity no longer neutralized threats to the social body by repressing libidinal excess—its diseased, feminized components. Instead, it sustained virtue and sexual potency and regulated moral order by removing repressive constraints on nature.

For example, in his study of German war veterans, Klaus Theweleit writes perceptively about their attitudes toward prostitutes:

> The entire complex of prostitution strikes a sensitive nerve in the patriarchal man, including the patriarchal man of the left. At stake are the purity and integrity of his sacred "organ," together with its outgrowth, his brain, itself also reaching ever upward. The patriarchal man of the left avoids the dangers of female sexuality (through castration or syphilis) by decreeing that in the class struggle there may be both men and women, but only one sex, that of the wage earner, which is to say, none at all. (1:167)

This passage demonstrates the distance between twentieth-century (primarily) middle-class German men and the Victorians. For the former, male sexuality—the sacred organ—is not distinct from but coextensive with the brain. The body and the mind are inseparable. Furthermore, male sexuality guarantees the coherence and rationality of the social body. If there is one sex that is no sex, it is because male sexuality has been cured of disease, restored to its "sacred integrity," and thus paradoxically purified of sexuality itself, of its fluidity and equation with self-loss and corporeal fragmentation— of its equation with women.

In his 1922 journal, the revolutionary German playwright Bertolt Brecht contrasted his own straightforward, virile sexuality with that of the woman who disappointed him and rid herself of their "illegitimate" fetus. He sought to save a poor actress from a loveless marriage to an industrialist, to restore her purity and integrity:

> This is how she repays me. . . . Everything . . . was just playacting under the stagelights, to the tune of coffeehouse music. . . . I've never seen such a naked display of the prostitute's bag of tricks, of her romanticism. So that's how a pregnant whore unloads! And to think I wanted to place that cracked pot in my room, when it was dripping with the discharges of every man around! Being abandoned, seen for what she is, unmasked. . . . That's the reason for her frightened rages. (quoted in Theweleit, 1:164)

Theweleit rightly points out that the image Brecht accused the actress of projecting was actually his own invention. Theweleit implies that this psychic logic—although due in part to feelings of inadequacy—was also part of a common cultural narrative that informs left-wing revolutionary discourse and fascism alike. Women's sexuality represents an illusion, and the man who succumbs loses his reason and his very selfhood: he is reduced to "every man around," as if his sexuality were a machine built to service women's desires. Brecht implicitly contrasts the actress's performance with his own transparency—his own virile integrity. His projection perpetuates the myth of a binary opposition between purity and impurity.

This same logic is apparent in the new cult of the body expressed in the *Nacktkultur* (nudist) and modern dance movements in Germany, as well as in the new emphasis on health and beauty in Britain. Peter Toepfer argues that in Weimar Germany nudity was conceived as a sign of modernity because it liberated the body from conventional cultural constraints.[14] At the same time the liberated body was not conceived as seductive but as the expression of nature in its primeval purity and transparency. Heinrich Pudor, who invented the term *Nacktkultur*, was an extreme right-wing thinker who sought to protest the confusion between nudism and pornography (Mosse, 48–49): nude bodies did not promise false gratification or create seductive illusions, at least not in theory.

In England the Women's League of Health and Beauty combined exhibition of the body with purity and health. The league allowed women to "dissociate the cultivation of physical beauty from narcissistic vanity and abandon."[15] In other words, women could attend to their bodies without the stigma of acting like women—that is, without the desire to adorn and hence seduce, to create an illusion in which men might lose themselves. The league created a cultural space within which women could enjoy their bodies and "have fun" (Matthews, 33, 48); it provided a way for women to experience their sexuality "respectably," purged of its seductive and hence feminine effects. While the league expressed the new unconstrained attitude to the body, the body was nevertheless permitted to shed its constraints only if purified—that is to say, defeminized.

Male Sexuality, Homosexuality, and Social Order

I argued earlier that the instability of gender boundaries after the Great War forced elite men to redefine gender difference. The sexual revolution that followed rendered male sexuality continuous with rather than opposed to social order, and the ideology of the liberated body redefined sexual liberation as the purification (defeminization) of the sexual subject. I think this is what Theweleit might mean when he says that during the interwar years there was one sex that was no sex: for the first time men equated sexuality exclusively with male sexuality. The sexual revolution made this equation possible because its most powerful advocates purged male sexuality of any traces of femininity—that is to say, of sexuality as it had been conventionally defined. Sexual revolutionaries turned femininity into the extension of masculinity, rather than into its "other." Hence, for example, British women who wanted to celebrate and enjoy their bodies felt pressure to purge them of all seductive effects in order to do so, and participants in the new celebration of unconstrained bodily movement—whether modern dancers or nudists— regimented and desexed their bodies in the process.

In keeping with this defeminization of the social body, democratic men demonized fascism by associating it with male homosexuality. Again and again, before and after World War Two, democrats cast aspersions on fascists by equating them with perverts. Wilhelm Reich, the prominent sexologist, made the absurd claim in 1927 that most homosexuals supported the war and most heterosexuals—or those who had "fully sublimated" their sexuality—opposed it (quoted in Theweleit, 54). Like Ellis, Reich claimed that giving free reign to sexual expression would eliminate homosexuality and pornography and help men to reclaim pure, restrained, and healthy, or sublimated manliness.[16] Later, in 1949, Arthur Schlesinger argued that totalitarian political systems were "psychoses" that offered "profound political appeal" but "pervert politics" into "something secret . . . and furtive . . . like homosexuality in a boys' school."[17]

Sympathy with fascist politics has long been equated in a famous cliche with either latent or overt homosexuality.[18] In fascist rhetoric, the individual merges with the totality (the nation); both the individual and public will are transparent and embodied in the figure of a charismatic leader. Scholars since Freud who have analyzed fascism's affective dimension speak of the "feminine" longing for authority and libidinal connection with the leader, as well as the sadomasochistic quality of the relationship between leader and people.[19] This sadomasochistic desire for authority and annihilation in the nation mirrors the de-differentiation putatively sought by homosexuals in their regressive, sadomasochistic, and narcissistic conflation of self and other. Unlike the individuated, healthy, and restrained democratic man, fascist men's pathological love of discipline reveals their emasculation, their need to prove they are real men because they are, as Theodor Adorno put it in *Minima Moralia* (1970), the "true effeminates" (quoted in Theweleit, 55).

These efforts to explain fascism as the product of (repressed) pathology—equating it with the very "perversion" it repudiates, homosexuality—again suggests that "healthy," democratic social order is symbolically masculine, purged of the regression, "secrecy" and sadomasochism implicitly associated with effeminate men and thus with femininity. According to these writers' logic, if we repress men's sexuality, we produce perverts—here homosexual men—and thereby risk perverting politics. The association these commentators established between homosexuality and fascism not only places sexuality at the heart of politics—healthy sexuality leads to democracy and perverted sexuality leads to fascism—it presumes that repression leads to perversion and suggests that the sexually liberated male body was, paradoxically, as Reich saw it, a (phantasmic) purified, defeminized body.

What were the effects of this paradox? Essentially, as I suggested earlier, it defines the way in which gender difference was restored in new terms—through sexual revolution, through the liberation of male sexuality. As the interwar development of a language of sexual equality demonstrates, masculinity had lost the natural foundations on which it had always rested, and the proponents of "real" manliness had to create its meaning while insisting they were only restoring manhood. Elite men thus defended their privilege by reinventing manhood ("nature") itself—by rendering male sexuality compatible with—indeed, continuous with—social order. Male sexuality was no longer "like" unrestrained female sexuality: an intrinsically anarchic drive which had to be repressed and regulated for the sake of social order. Liberated male sexuality was "natural"—pure—sexuality, and social order was the expression of this nature. Although this logic is hard to follow, critics of all sorts rendered restrained, healthy male sexuality the consequence of de-repression.

Sexual Equality and Social Order

After the war, the backlash expressed by critics and in popular novels testified to a world in which gender roles had been inverted and irrevocably changed, as if mourning for a lost world were itself testimony to the naturalness or "truth" of the foundations on which social order had once rested. Even sexual reformers believed the natural foundations of healthy heterosexuality had been compromised by the repressiveness of Victorian marriage. Remember that conservatives and reformers alike narrated the new woman's challenge to normative gender roles as either the permanent inversion of nature (Lièvre) or its restoration (Verone, Stopes, Ellis): reformers finally preserved the idea of natural order by transforming the meaning of nature itself.

One hundred and fifty years after the French Revolution, the new commitment to equality included women even as it continued to exclude them. Most men with democratic beliefs gave women the vote, but their power-sharing was consistent with the regulation of female sexuality. Dissident voices had difficulty using the language of sexual equality to demand real equality, since the widespread presumption was that heterosexual male sexuality was most compatible with social order and social justice. Thus, we might chart the historical transformation of sexual relations in terms of gendered selves that had lost their moral or natural foundation and hence were always subject to change. We might thus question how the relationship between gender and sexuality has been constituted, by whom, and through what powers and institutions.

5

Sexuality, Obscenity Law, and Violence in the United States: 1950–1994

[Pornography] breeds lust. Lust defiles the body, debauches the imagination, corrupts the mind, deadens the will, destroys the memory, sears the conscience, hardens the heart, and damns the soul.

—Anthony Comstock

Violence and death have saved us from sex.

—G. Legman, *Love and Death* (1963)

In the late nineteenth and early twentieth centuries, both advocates and opponents of censorship sought to preserve a social body that would be, after the human form it idealized, impermeable, productive, and emotionally and physically self-contained. By the interwar years harsh forms of repression had been discredited in favor of sexual liberation. Through the complex process I described in chapters 3 and 4, male sexuality became, paradoxically, coextensive with virility, corporeal integrity, and containment. Sexual liberals celebrated the naturalness of heterosexual desire and relegated all other desires to the category of the "obscene." In both western Europe and North America that category represented—and still represents—an effort to contain threats to stable selfhood defined in terms of normative masculinity and normative heterosexual expression.

Although obscenity and pornography are not synonymous (obscenity is a broader term encompassing all "repugnant" representation), obscenity law in the United States is now applied mostly to sexually explicit material.[1] The application of obscenity law varies from one culture to the next; Sweden has abolished censorship entirely. Nevertheless, whether real or rhetorical, in all Western industrialized countries, birth control information and various sorts of dissident literature have ceased to be designated as obscenity, which now targets primarily homosexuality and sometimes nonnormative heterosexual practices. Moreover, texts once condemned for obscenity are increasingly exempt from prosecution as their content has been judged "healthy" according to new standards informed by the discourse on de-repression.

As early as 1926 a French judge declared that materials could be justly prosecuted if they "constituted an apology for pederasty, sought to arouse homosexual passions and to provoke unwholesome curiosity."[2] In 1930 another French judge claimed that books describing relations with prostitutes should be prime targets of the law. Although in 1940, 1955, and 1958, special pleas and provisions were established for erotic books and books written in a "creative spirit"—that is, not solely for commercial gain—and antipornography legislation was broadened by 1958 to encompass "films, photographs, and photographic reproductions" (Bécourt, 85–86). The 1958 law reconciled earlier laws that prohibited obscenity because of the presumed need to "defend" the family and children (1939 and 1949, respectively) with the protection of certain categories of texts deemed literary.

In England legislators reinforced the Obscene Publications Act in 1959 to address the laxity of modern media and to protect the family and children from "unwholesome representations." However, in *Regina v. Penguin Books* (1960), judges sought to protect D. H. Lawrence's *Lady Chatterly's Lover* and other literature by arguing that a book should not be conceived in terms of isolated prurient passages but as an aesthetic whole. According to one text, "witness after witness instructed the court in *Regina vs. Penguin Books* on how to discipline the self by confronting the secret truth of sex."[3] These witnesses replicated the interwar argument that reconciled discipline and sexuality and defined disciplined sexuality as male sexuality. Implicitly, they identified great literature with disciplined masculinity, and pornography, once again, with consumer culture and uncontrolled femininity.

Although most highbrow literature is now relatively safe from prosecution, dissident sexuality remains a primary focus of censorship laws. In 1987 the powerful French politician Jacques Chirac expressed his concern over explicit homosexual images. In the United States the infamous Helms Amendment (1989), sponsored by Republican Senator Jesse Helms, sought to prohibit representations of homosexuality and sadomasochism. In England the Conservative majority aimed its wrath at homosexual images and behavior and sponsored Section 28 (of the Local Government Act) in 1988 to prohibit local authorities from "intentionally promoting homosexuality."[4]

In this chapter I focus on obscenity because it is not only a gauge of how sexual regulation functions and who it affects but because debates about obscenity presume that sexuality can be defined and shaped by words and images—that supposedly biologically determined practices, paradoxically, are above all a matter of culture. Moreover, with some exceptions, scholars do not conventionally treat pornography as a changing historical phenomenon (unlike recent works on abortion or homosexuality), because sexual fantasy has been and still is for the most part constructed as ahistorical— as a product of the free imagination or as the perverse fantasies of deviants.

From European to American Feminist Discourses about Sexuality

Far more than its European counterpart, the American antipornography movement has been assimilated into mainstream discourse and continues to inform obscenity legislation. Western European feminist movements have generally been allied with working-class parties or internally divided along ideological lines. The American focus on individual rights permitted an exclusive focus on women's needs and demands and encouraged debate about female sexuality (and femininity) more generally.

In Europe women have benefited from the more developed welfare state (whether it was intended to benefit women or not), which has given them access to prenatal and general medical care, state subsidized child care, and family allocations. Many state policies had been implemented (and later dismantled) after the Great War, but the requirements of sustaining workforces, repopulating devastated nations, and redressing discrimination against women and workers after the Second World War required an interventionist state. The devastation wrought by the war made welfare subsidies necessary, and the sense of shared struggle against Nazi oppression in England, France, and Italy gave politicians the political will to enact progressive legislation in many areas. The English and Italian governments both mandated equal pay for equal work, although such legislation remained primarily rhetorical, especially during the cold war. Employment patterns changed by the mid-1960s and 1970s, including the increased participation of married women in the labor force, but women's salaries were still not equal to men's. Moreover, welfare provisions were gendered, especially in England: the state presumed a male breadwinner in each family and refused to make subsidy payments to married women. Even in France, where subsidies were apportioned on an individual basis, the state's leaders sought to assimilate women into traditional roles.[5]

In Italy and France women finally won the right to vote, in part because of the important roles they played in the Resistance. Nevertheless, fear of population decline led politicians to reassert traditional gender roles. General Charles de Gaulle made his famous call for "twelve million healthy babies" upon his return to France. To inspire higher rates of childbirth by stigmatizing women who deviated from normal gender roles, the West German government promoted the "natural" male-headed family, a denial of postwar reality. Most West German families were headed by women because so many men had been slaughtered.[6]

Finally, a new sexual revolution began in the mid-1960s with the increasing availability of contraceptives and the development of birth control technology (the pill). The sexual revolution of the sixties was inseparable from the growing consumer culture spawned by postwar economic prosperity. That culture's transformation of sexuality into a product available to everyone was facilitated by and anticipated in new, glossy sex magazines like *Playboy* and its international imitators, which offered women as objects of consumption and encouraged men to shed traditional family responsibilities to pursue sexual pleasure.[7] The historian Bonnie Smith has argued that this new emphasis on men's sexual prowess and freedom was in part compensation for their lack of the technological skills the modern world increasingly required; such a focus implicitly put greater responsibility on women for children. Furthermore, women consumed but did not produce birth control technology and so had little say in determining how, when, and to whom it would be made available.[8] Contraceptives may have become increasingly accessible to middle-class white women, but women's demand for them was always balanced with the needs of the state in regard to population. This lack of power is especially evident in the struggle for abortion rights, which were finally granted in France in 1975, in Italy in 1978, in the United States in 1973, and in Germany only when a doctor deemed the operation medically or psychologically necessary.

Historians have often noted that women's liberation grew out of middle-class white women's disillusionment with their left-wing brothers in struggle. In student and worker uprisings in Paris and Berkeley in 1968, women found themselves excluded from positions of real responsibility by men who preached gender and sexual equality. Moreover, they began to question the benefits they had reaped from the sexual revolution. Their critiques of the enduring double standard—men played around, women still suffered the moral and medical consequences—engendered a new language for women to use in speaking about their sexuality. In spite of national and cultural differences, women's movements everywhere challenged the new sexual mores and the traditional gender roles and expectations on which they continued to be based. They criticized the notion that women's inferior status represented individual failure rather than institutionalized discrimination.

By the mid-1970s, especially as abortion rights were granted, women's movements began to focus on complex issues such as images of women in the media, and thus on women and consumer culture more generally. The concept of women as objects had been a primary concern of early women's liberationists; in France, Britain, and the United States, women challenged the traditional images of femininity perpetuated everywhere from beauty contests to women's magazines. Nevertheless, in contrast to the United States (and to a lesser extent, Great Britain), Western European feminists had little success addressing women's concerns specifically as women's concerns. Politically successful rhetoric about women's oppression has been generally confined, at least since the early years of women's liberation, to the language of socioeconomic marginality. Claire Duchen provides an exceptionally astute account of the internal divisions within the French women's movement produced by women's commitment to the Left. The French Socialist

Party marginalized women's demands or reframed them as class or "family" issues. For example, the struggle for abortion rights was waged as a class struggle to make abortion as available to working-class women as it was to their bourgeois counterparts, who could afford illegal ones.[9]

Although addressing socioeconomic concerns has had many real advantages for some women, European feminists have not posed the same challenge to normative sexuality as their American sisters have; there is little discussion of sexual harassment, lesbian and gay rights, or the social effects of pornography (or at least, their positions have remained relatively marginal). On 21 December 1994 the British left-wing newspaper *The Guardian* ran an article on sexual harassment on college campuses; it did not offer a feminist perspective, not even as a foil for those opposed to "politically correct" positions. The article even contained a warning to readers against following the American example of attempting to control something as intangible as heterosexual relations.

In the former West Germany and France, there have been feminist attacks on pornography, but their impact has been muted. German works often call the antipornography feminist movement in their own country an "import from the United States."[10] Although the antipornography movement made headway in 1986—when the editor of the feminist magazine *Emma* began what was dubbed the "PorNo" campaign—its force abated when the major political parties, which had at first shown some interest in the movement, took little action. In 1987, women politicians from the center-right Christian Democrats (*CDU*) sought with antipornography feminists to draft a bill fashioned after an American antipornography feminist ordinance which defined pornography as a violation of women's rights. But according to a history by activist Bettina Bremme, none of the law's women advocates in parliament would openly announce their support, and no action was ever taken.[11]

In 1984, when French cabinet member Yvette Roudy sponsored legislation prohibiting sexual discrimination, equivalent to racial discrimination laws already on the books, she was openly mocked for her "puritanism" by left-wing newspapers and by men and women alike. Most of the controversy revolved around her effort to censor images deemed "degrading" to women.[12]

I thus focus on feminist debates about sexuality and pornography in the United States after 1980 because American feminists have most dramatically conceived pornography as intertwined with historical questions concerning gender and power. American feminists opposed to pornographic images have replicated older concerns about sexuality as polluting, contagious, and self-fragmenting, as if impermeable, integral female subjects are the new combat veterans of a war whose generals have dehumanized them and seduced them into acting against their own best interests. My analysis will demonstrate to what extent even adversarial feminist analyses of sexuality and its history are infused with images of contaminated, fragmented bodies.

Framing the American Feminist Debate

Activists and intellectuals involved in defending or celebrating pornography agree that sexuality is everywhere, that it is "spreading," that it is always on display for better or for worse in explicit and sometimes insidious forms, and that the proliferation of sexually explicit material is the most visible symptom of sexuality's pervasiveness. In a recent article, the film critic Linda Williams writes: "An older era of American jurisprudence could more simply dismiss a range of sexual representations that were presumably only 'for sex's sake'—that is, just for purposes of arousal. But this definition has gradually changed as 'sex' has become an increasingly important motive force, so entwined with all aspects of human desire and endeavor as to be difficult to isolate in an absolutely pure state of obscenity."[13]

The pervasiveness of sexuality is thus inextricable from the shifting functions and targets of obscenity law, which no longer simply regulates certain sexual practices but differentiates normal from pathological selves. Nowadays censors do not generally target texts and images that depict normative heterosexuality. Williams argues that in the United States the meaning of obscenity depends on sexual others—primarily nonheterosexuals and individuals who engage in sexual activities not consummated by heterosexual intercourse. She conceives censorship as an attack on the sexual diversity that undermines normative heterosexuality and thus normative masculinity and femininity as well. Censorship is also an attack on the presumed femininity of pornography's consumers, characterized by "satiety, passivity, absorption."[14]

Williams, among others, claims more specifically that obscenity law depends on a cultural narrative of self-control and on a teleology (heterosexual intercourse) threatened by "others." In late twentieth–century North America sexuality can no longer be isolated in a pure state, and some sexualities have become more socially acceptable than others. Although Williams describes rather than analyzes the historical shifts in the definition of obscenity, she does try to account for the complexity and mutability of the pornographic genre. Pornography is no hegemonic narrative aimed primarily at fulfilling heterosexual men's fantasies. "Other" sexualities work to transform the viewer's projected fantasies through shifting sexual identifications encouraged by the texts and images themselves.

Williams argues that pornography can be neither liberating nor dangerously contagious. Rather, pornography permits identifications and fantasies that proliferate out of the interaction between viewer and film or between reader and text, thus "polluting" in some fashion everyone who consumes it. Williams gives "contagion" an affirmative valuation, however: it signifies the insatiability and lack of narrative closure characteristic of all sexual desire. In other words, there is no liberation intrinsic in pornography, no repressed sexual "self" to be liberated, because there is no end to desire. The sexual self is perpetually in formation, perpetually experiencing itself in new ways. It has no foundation.

Williams still has a hard time explaining how pornography can both express social power (of men over women) and challenge or transform social norms. She cannot explain the relationship between changes within the genre (and hence within the viewer or reader) and changes in the broader cultural function of narratives about pornography. Changes within pornography itself focus on psychic processes; changes in its cultural function are related to social and cultural power, itself permeated by psychic dynamics but not reducible to them. Thus, while it can be said that the social and cultural function of pornography is to reinforce male hegemony, pornography is a very complex genre that defies such a reductive analysis.[15]

The question at hand is not whether pornography is good or bad. My concern is with how and why violence (and sadism in particular), with its boundary-dissolving, putatively contagious effects, has become linked to pornography in the United States since the 1950s, and how this vision of sexuality has shaped different attitudes toward obscenity law. I use the rhetorical link between sexuality and violence in its myriad forms to argue that censorship represents an effort to ward off threats to the concept of stable sexuality first defined in the interwar years and embedded in normative heterosexual expression.

Obscenity Legislation and Its Context

Sexual liberation was finally implanted in U.S. cultural mores by the end of World War II. The famous studies of male and female sexuality by the zoologist Alfred Kinsey appeared in 1948 and 1953, respectively, and revealed a wide range of sexual activities by American adults beneath an ideology of sexual normalcy and purity. Postwar social developments expressed more clearly than ever the paradox whereby women's sexuality was both permitted free expression (in women's magazines and in new mores among youth, for example) and channeled into procreation and the ideologically maintained private sphere.

Between 1940 and 1960 the proportion of married women in the labor force doubled from 15 to 30 percent, and the single working woman became a necessary part of the labor force because of the postwar expansion of the retail and service sectors. Helen Gurley Brown's *Cosmopolitan* urged women to enjoy sexual indulgence and autonomy, and the birth control pill made it possible for increasing numbers of women to control their fertility and thus to make new kinds of lives for themselves. A new singles culture developed in large urban areas, and more and more people were trying to sustain more liberal sexual relationships. It became more acceptable for women to engage in at least limited premarital sexual activity without compromising their reputations. The new courtship ritual of "going steady" legitimated women's sexual expression by placing it within the context of a heterosexual relationship that would presumably end in marriage (D'Emilio & Freedman, 302–10).

Yet as these changes eroded traditional family structures, ideology about normative gender roles became increasingly rigid. A rigid gender ideology was justified by a new ideology about the traditional family promulgated by the cold war: the family was the symbolic center of a stable, capitalist moral and social order—the crux of American strength against Communism. Men and women married and had children earlier. Advice books and hygiene lectures at universities emphasized the importance of not engaging in premarital sex and reinforced the double standard.

Elaine Tyler May has persuasively argued that the ideology of the traditional family emerged as a buffer against the new freedoms arising out of consumerism, technological innovation, women's economic and sexual emancipation, and urban life more generally. Although Americans recognized women's sexual and economic independence, they sought to channel women's energies into the family, where they could be domesticated and controlled. Women's sexuality outside the home (or inside if no male authority was present) symbolized danger and political subversion. May cites a civil defense pamphlet issued as late as 1972 that demonstrates the metaphorical association drawn between unrestrained female sexuality and the danger posed to America by atomic weapons: radioactive rays are depicted as attractive women—as "bombshells."[16] The ideology of the traditional family thus sought to harness women's sexuality in the interests of preserving American's freedom (May, 112). The family was a "psychological fortress that would protect [Americans] from themselves" (111), and domesticated women were its literal and symbolic center.

Many American legislators and citizens used censorship of materials they deemed obscene to shape this ideology of the family—that is, to regulate the family in new terms by making homosexuality and other non-normative heterosexual practices the primary targets of obscenity law. Indeed, obscenity law eventually exempted birth control literature, politically dissident work, and art and literature deemed to have aesthetic merit. This expansion of the definition of the non-obscene began in 1934 with Judge John Woolsey's ruling that James Joyce's *Ulysses* had to be judged in terms of its entire message rather than on the basis of isolated passages. In the 1957 case *Roth v. the United States*, the definition of obscenity was affirmed and yet refined: arguing that not all sexually explicit works fall outside First Amendment protection, Justice William Brennan acknowledged that sex is "a great and mysterious motive force in human life" and "has indisputably been a subject of absorbing interest to mankind through the ages."[17] Only pornographic material appealing to "prurient interest" (unhealthy sexuality) could be deemed obscene. Three criteria have been established since 1966 to define obscenity: a work must be "patently offensive"; it must appeal to "prurient interest"; and it must be "utterly without redeeming social value." *Miller v. California* (1973) affirmed these criteria but emphasized the distinction between works that do and do not have "serious value," making it easier to prosecute works with no pretensions to "literary, artistic, political, or scientific value." (Downs, 17)[18]

This expansion of the legal definitions of the non-obscene was accompanied by a backlash against sexual expression that underscored the vagueness of those definitions. During the cold war, anti-Communists pointed (once again) to obscenity, homosexuality, and deviant women as signs of the moral decay that was draining the nation's ability to fight communism from within and without. Perverted sexuality was no longer equated solely with "others" but was potentially and dangerously everywhere. According to John D'Emilio and Estelle Freedman, the image of the obscenity peddler was no longer an immigrant, but any respectable citizen, even a white, "rather characterless" (284) male suburbanite.[19]

Moreover, pornography preyed above all on innocent children, future soldiers in the war against communism. In 1952 the House of Representatives authorized an investigation of popular paperbacks to judge their effects on youth. By the end of the 1950s, 14 states had tightened obscenity laws to cover the sale of comic books in particular, although antiobscenity organizations had targeted other sorts of popular entertainment and even some high-culture texts as well. The American Book Publishers Council reported that "decent literature drives" were held in 35 U.S. counties during the winter of 1957–58, and in 1959 the postmaster general claimed the government arrested more people that year for mailing obscenity than had ever been recorded before (Loth, 43). As evidenced by the concern with "sexually suggestive" comic books, pornography was equated above all with juvenile delinquency and the decay of youth's moral fiber. One congressional report claimed there might be a "connection between pornographic literature and subversive elements" (D'Emilio and Freedman, 282).

The connection was more clearly spelled out by a Philadelphia antivice crusader explaining the dangers of sexually explicit material: "Girls run away from their homes and become entangled in prostitution. Boys and young men who have difficulty resisting the undue sexual stimulation become sexually aggressive and generally incorrigible. The more vicious . . . may become an exhibitionist, a rapist, a sadist, a fetishist. He may commit such antisocial acts as arson, pyromania, and kleptomania, which are often symbolic sexual acts" (quoted in D'Emilio and Freedman, 284). This observer assumes that the less developed a young person's self-control, the more damaging exposure to pornography will be. He also presumes through his (vulgar) psychoanalytic allusions that antisocial violent behavior is the expression of sexual impulses gone awry. He blames the contagious nature of sexual texts and images and their ability to contaminate those not yet immunized by healthy psychosexual development.[20]

The language of contagion was also used in the discourse about homosexuality during this period. In December 1950 the Senate committee assigned to investigate homosexuals in the government concluded that they lacked "emotional stability" and were morally weakened by sexual indulgence. The report implied that homosexuality was contagious, that "perverts" "polluted" those who came into contact with them, and that homosexuals were particularly dangerous when allowed contact with "young and impressionable people" (quoted in D'Emilio and Freedman, 293). Censors targeted Allen Ginsberg's *Howl* because of its homosexual content as well as its celebration of the "freer" sexuality of blacks. By 1953 more and more homosexuals were being purged from the armed forces, and President Eisenhower issued an executive order that year banning gay men and lesbians from all federal employment (D'Emilio and Freedman, 275–300).

Once again, then, the liberalization of sexuality (at least of sexually explicit words and images) went in tandem with increased sexual regulation. Once again, the primary targets of regulation were people symbolically associated with femininity and the destabilization of gender norms. And once again, this paradoxical association of liberalization with regulation characterized not only the political Right but the Left as well. Critics on both sides quibbled less about sexuality per se than about its forms. They did not disagree about what was normal and what was perverse; instead, they disagreed about how to go about shaping a normal, healthy society. Moreover, since sexual mores had shifted so profoundly since the 1920s, antivice crusaders of the 1960s no longer represented a mainstream view of sexuality. As a result, new sorts of anticensorship narratives had more influence on popular opinion and more clearly mirrored the paradoxes underlying shifting mores.

Sexual Reformers and Censorship

I have already documented the shift in the relationship between masculinity and social order, a shift that had permitted social purification, paradoxically, through the release of male libido. The emergence of a structurally similar yet substantively different discourse about pornography and censorship in the early 1960s—the left-wing narratives opposing censorship—exemplifies the failure of the older narrative to sustain fully the impermeable boundaries of the phallic, purified self. Proliferating forms of mass entertainment, the anxieties produced by consumer culture (well documented in John Kenneth Galbraith's *The Affluent Society*), a perceived increase in perversion and Stalinism (as well as memories of fascism), all threatened in new ways to contaminate virile selfhood.[21]

Like their counterparts in the twenties and thirties, sexual liberals (for lack of a better term) in the early 1960s believed that free speech about sexuality guaranteed social stability. They, too, conceived that stability in terms of an authentic selfhood embedded in normative heterosexuality. In a remarkable shift whose origins and outlines I have already sketched, these commentators opposed Anthony Comstock's nineteenth-century assertion that sadism was the consequence of unbridled sexuality.[22] Instead, they believed repressed sexuality caused sadism. Some argued that free sexual expression was a safety valve that spared society the violence that repressed sexuality produced. Debates about censorship in this period were not only about defining obscenity but about the distinction between normal sexual expression and obscene or "pornographic" sexuality.

G. Legman's radical, left-wing anticensorship diatribe *Love and Death* (1963) is worth examining in detail because it is a dramatic example of this kind of literature.[23] Legman gives no reason why only sadism can replace sex except tautologically by reference to the high level of violence in the U.S. media. According to Legman, this level of violence marks the displacement of sexuality and signals a refusal to accept it as natural and in need of an outlet. Here he parts from the moralists who took a more Comstockian view (that too much sexuality is dangerous) without Comstock's prudery: they believed public sexual expression is acceptable within certain limits. Legman argued that violence, or displaced sexuality, is seductive and all-encompassing. The murder mystery, for example, literally halts rational thought processes: it functions as a safety valve that pacifies its consumers because they "do" in fantasy what they cannot do in reality. "Does your boss tyrannize and exploit you? Don't shoot him—you'll hang for it. Kill him nightly on paper—you the detective, he the hounded-down murderer" (22). Legman argues that reading this kind of material—reading about violence—is no different from doing it: "Make no mistake about it: the mystery reader is a lyncher" (16). Legitimate anger is never resolved (by social change, for example) but continually displaced in phantasmic identifications that must be continually reenacted: hence we require more and more violence.

The figures of the "bitch-heroine" and the "pansy intellectual" who forfeits his natural virility are produced by the unresolved, uncontained, and finally emasculating rage specific to murder mysteries. It should come as no surprise that the writers of murder mysteries are "pansy intellectuals, homicidal housewives, and pseudonymous college professors" (23). These writers and their dangerous books compromise the natural ritual of courtship because the "normal sadism" involved in courtship—male pursuit, the cruel coyness of women—becomes sex itself: foreplay replaces consummation. The bitch-heroine moves from the pages of fiction into the real world, and her sadistic treatment of men replaces normal sexual relations. Legman notes, for example, the claim by Ben Ames, author of the popular novel *The Strange Woman*, that the sadistic, murderous heroines he intended to contain overwhelmed all his efforts: Ames wrote that "the central character usurped that book and to some extent defeated its original intent" (quoted in Legman, 63).

Not surprisingly, the degeneration of normal sexual relations through this perversion of gender norms is most explicitly and dangerously conveyed by an insidious homosexuality—inseparable, in Legman's view, from creeping fascism. The predominance of "pansies and housewives" in shaping cultural mores was symptomatic of the pervasive, uncontained femininity draining the manliness necessary for rational thought and social change. Indeed, modern culture is a war between two forms of virility: one real, one feigned ("faggotry"). Children who identify with outlaws of all sorts "consummate [their] Oedipean dream of strength" and become real men because they "break through [their environment]," become their own person. But

> the Supermen, the Supersleuths, the Supercops do not. They align themselves always on the side of law, authority, the father; and accept their power passively from a bearded above. They are not competing—not for the forbidden mother, not for any other reward. Like Wild Bill Hickok, our own homosexual hero out thar where men were men—with his . . . Lesbian side-kick, Calamity Jane—they are too unvirile to throw off fear, and kill as criminals. Instead, unseen and unsuspected in some corner, they put on a

> black mask, a sheriff's badge and a Superman suit, and do
> all their killing on the side of the law. (43)

Thus, the latent homosexuality in Superman is dangerous because
it encourages men to overcompensate for their "evasion of the real
conflict [between father and son] in endless repetition of the symbolic death [of the father]" (79). Although homosexuals act like "real
men," they are really fearful, like lesbians and all frigid women.
Superman is a fascist in disguise, and the sexually repressed readers
of comic strips become no different from the Nazis who gassed Jews
(13–14).

The repression of sexuality leads to sadism, which leads to homosexuality, emasculation, fascism, and the end of the struggle for
social justice. The absence of normative heterosexuality perpetuates
social injustice by allowing febrile, unstable selves to long, like
fascists, for the narcissistic dissolution of distinctions (and hence of
conflicts) between self and other. They long, in other words, for an
infantile omnipotence in the absence of "others" to set limits, and
hence they endlessly search for symbolic death in a fantasy world
where they alone can be sovereign.

Sexual Reformers and Homosexuality

The sexual liberals' notion that repressed sexuality led to social
instability was also expressed in a more moderate book, *The Homosexual Revolution* (1962). Its author, R. E. Masters, claimed that "our
society's refusal to permit the honest treatment of sexual relationships is directly responsible for much of our preoccupation with
violence and cruelty."[24] Censorship in all its forms "transmutes
desire into death." Although it does not make a direct equation
between homosexuality and fascism, this book implies that censorship is the tool of the weak, of "sex-obsessed alchemists" (134). In
other words, the displacement of sex into violence perverts sex
itself, prevents it from developing in a healthy, normal fashion.
Like Legman, Masters cites two inextricably linked consequences
of this development: the emancipation of women and the emasculation of men. Although he makes no effort to predict the "unfortu-
nate" results of this inevitable "upset" of the "psychological and
emotional and sexual balance between males and females" (185),
and although he generally preaches tolerance for homosexuals, his
narrative retains homosexuals as the villains in a war between real

manliness and the dreadful, emasculating effects of the consumer culture engulfing cold war America.

This demonization of male homosexuals (lesbians are only a secondary focus) is most evident in his invocation of "homosexual panic," identified as a psychological disorder in 1920 but not codified until 1952 in the *Diagnostic and Statistical Manual of the Psychiatric Profession*.[25] Masters notes that so many men have latent homosexual tendencies that, out of fear and in defense, they do violence to openly or suspected homosexual men. Struggling to celebrate sexuality and yet to free it from contagion and perversion, the author condemns not homophobia but the contagion of homosexuality. On the most literal level, he believes all children exposed to homosexuals will become homosexual (131). This emphasis on homosexuality's contagion rather than on homophobia accords with the logic of homosexual panic. The "disorder" presumes that homosexuality is latent in large numbers of men for whom homosexual feelings provoke defenses ranging from what the psychiatrist Burton Glick called "vague feelings of discomfort to truly horrifying fright accompanied by disordered thought and behavior" (quoted in Comstock, 83).[26] In the 1960s the legal profession began to use homosexual panic as a legal defense for men who assaulted homosexuals. As both doctors and lawyers conceived it, the assailant was finally less to blame than the homosexual, who evoked anxiety through the "hypnotic effects" of his perverted sexuality.[27]

In spite of Masters's sympathy for the assailant, he contends that the man who reacts with violence out of fear that he might be homosexual does display unmanly behavior, and that his excessive violence is inimical to social order: such latent feelings cause a "very serious disturbance of self control." The psychiatric literature shows, moreover, that these latent homosexuals often do not actually suffer from violence but hallucinate attacks against them: "A patient might complain that 'someone is throwing voices' into his head, making him hear voices, have visions, making him have a peculiar taste in his mouth, putting poison in his food, shooting electricity into his body, hypnotizing him, going to kill, crucify, initiate him, or make him join a society or religion, or steal his manhood, etc." (Comstock, 85). Although Masters claims that homosexual panic and its consequences are "understandable" (165), the identification of straight men with gay men and the confusion of self and other this identification suggests signifies an intolerable lack of restraint and femininity characteristic of homosexuals, whose narcissism "is catching. One has to repeatedly come up for air, get away from the sickly sweet vapors that befog the mind" (23). Here, the repression of sexuality leads to the spread of homosexual tendencies throughout the population (even though the panic defense assumes they are already there), leading in turn to sadism. Masters's attitude toward the homosexual panic defense is ambivalent: it recognizes the pervasiveness of homosexuality and signifies the emasculation of a culture driven to unrestrained and irrational violence (the specter of fascism looming on the horizon) by homosexuals' "sweet vapors." Thus, he repudiates censorship but fears the feminizing effects of unrestrained sexuality.

Free speech, paradoxically, does not permit diverse sexual expression; rather, it guarantees social justice, sexual health, proper gender roles, and the self-restrained autonomy of truly virile men. Masters, trying to remain a pluralist in spite of his ambivalence, does not condemn homosexuals explicitly for inciting attacks on themselves, but he does ask that we give vice squad members and detectives "special training in psychology . . . with only the mentally and emotionally stable being permitted to work in these important areas" (165). Only normal, heterosexual, self-contained men—the least likely to succumb to homosexuals' hypnotic power—need apply for these jobs.

In spite of their different points of view, Legman's *Love and Death* and Masters's *The Homosexual Revolution* repeat the same themes. They are representative of the literature about censorship and perversion produced in the late fifties and early sixties. This literature used homosexuality as the privileged expression of a nonconsummated sexuality and, in so doing, distinguished between normative and non-normative forms of sexual expression as well as normal and deviant models of selfhood. Most important, it did so from a point of view opposed to censorship.[28]

Pornography and Self-Division

Other contemporaneous discussions of pornography do not privilege homosexuality in this fashion but do distinguish between normal sexuality and pornography on the basis of its presumed aim (or aimlessness). Normal sexuality is relational, intersubjective, a process of self-loss that guarantees self-discovery. Pornography is antisocial, like masturbation: it implies self-loss with no purpose. In these texts, pornography replaces prostitution as the primary drain on an otherwise healthy, vigorous, and productive society because pornography best symbolizes the dangerously feminizing effects of consumer culture (and less explicitly, the emasculating, libidinal relationship between a charismatic leader and his male followers).

Following D. H. Lawrence's example, the anthropologist Margaret Mead repudiated the notion that pornography might be a social safety valve. In 1953 she noted that, unlike bawdy jokes, pornography stimulates feelings "independent of another" and thus has no social function.[29] In fact, in *Continuities in Cultural Evolution* (1964), she claims that pornography bears "the signature of nonparticipation—of the dreaming adolescent, the frightened, the impotent, the bored and sated. . . . [It] evoke[s] and feed[s] an impulse that has no object" (quoted in Peckham, 25). She thus asserts that pornography is antisocial because it stands in for a relationship (as sadism replaces sex). Moreover, she draws on the standard vocabulary of those who criticized the emasculating effects of consumer culture—dreams, fear, impotence, boredom, and so forth. Finally, Steven Marcus's famous *The Other Victorians* (1964), although notable for attempting to historicize pornography, uses a psychoanalytic model in which the act of pornographic consumption is itself regressive and antisocial. Marcus conceives the use of pornography as a necessary "stage" in a developmental process toward psychosexual maturity; nevertheless, the pleasure derived from its consumption is an immature form of sexual gratification.[30]

In 1969 the scholar Morse Peckham argued that, since no one can be neutral about pornography, each critic's definition will inevitably reflect his or her concept of sexual normalcy. Peckham rightly located Mead's, Lawrence's, and Marcus's anxieties about pornography in their fear that its use dissolves clear boundaries between subjects and objects: "To treat one's own body, therefore, as in masturbation, as a sexual object is to do exactly what one does in treating another organism's body as a sexual object. To treat another personality as a sexual object is identical with treating one's own personality as a sexual object" (26). He argues that this self-objectification and hence self-division (treating one's self as an object) is not socially dangerous but socially useful. "If the body of the daydreamer and the personality of the daydreamer [the consumer of pornography] are indeed other, then the way is open to asserting that mental activity can serve the interests of others *because* it serves the individual's interests" (27).

Peckham also argues that pornography functions as a safety valve because it drains energies that might be expressed in other antisocial behavior. Although the murders of Martin Luther King Jr. and John F. Kennedy were hardly desirable, they gave some people, he suggests, the satisfaction of grieving in a publicly sanctioned fashion, and others the satisfaction of expressing hostility (by refusing to mourn) they might otherwise have acted out in dangerous ways. The assassinations allowed for the displacement and catharsis of powerful antisocial emotions. Like assassinations, pornography neutralizes the violence in the sexual emotions it stimulates. Unlike Mead and others, Peckham holds that the self-division (or self-objectification) inherent in reading pornography does not mark the self's narcissism, emasculation, or homosexuality but consolidates social order, paradoxically, by sustaining the boundaries between self and other.

Peckham's work reflects more directly than other discussions the stakes involved in narratives for and against sexual liberation from the interwar years to the 1960s. Recall that interwar discourses about sexual liberation paradoxically sought to purify sexuality and channel it into normal healthy outlets. American narratives about pornography were equally paradoxical, and as in the interwar years, their paradoxical premises arose out of fear of self-loss and self-fragmentation—above all, the fear that uncontained sexuality would lead to the dissolution of a unified, coherent, phallic self. Peckham also explicitly acknowledges the division intrinsic in male subjectivity. His work is the first text I have located that self-consciously articulates the anxiety-inducing effects of pornography in terms of self-objectification and hence self-division.

But like his interwar and more recent predecessors, Peckham both acknowledges and erases self-division. He never explains why the divided self provides the foundation for a unified one, and hence why and how using pornography actually contains the antisocial impulses it stimulates. Again, pornography, which functions here as a synecdoche for sexuality, is only acceptable to the extent that its effects are antipornographic—to the extent that masturbation consolidates healthy sexuality. Peckham implicitly repudiates the standard rhetoric about homosexuality invoked by Legman, Masters, and even indirectly by Mead (who links pornography to impotence, fear, and satiation, the same words used to describe the causes and effects of homosexuality). For them, homosexuality is bad, antisocial sexuality. It threatens the cohesiveness of the self, but not because same-sex desire has no object. Instead, like the narcissist (or the masturbator, for that matter), the homosexual subject takes itself as an object and so fails to secure boundaries between self and other. The self is fluid, internally divided, and, as Legman saw it, "unvirile." Normal, healthy sexuality requires two coherent subjects to form a union with a social function, aim, and teleology. Peckham believes that pornography produces real men, not perverted ones, but he is unable to explain how self-division produces real men instead of emasculated, fearful ones who compensate for their "lack" with the fantasy of unrestrained sovereign power. His argument is thus finally difficult to differentiate from the narrative that conceives nonphallic (emasculated, homosexual, feminine) sexuality as a dangerous, antisocial form of self-division that leads to male impotence at best and fascism at worst.

Women's Liberation and the Antipornography Movement

This cultural anxiety about nonphallic sexuality formed the framework for the new wave of procensorship campaigns that emerged in the late 1970s and early 1980s. In the earlier two decades, the threat of communism had legitimated the purge of people, texts, and images judged to be undermining the American family and hence American virility. Obscene material was the symbolic (and for some, the literal) intersection of the unconstrained violence and sexuality that threatened to contaminate American culture. The censorship forces of the 1970s and 1980s represented a backlash against the presumed sexual liberation of the 1960s, as well as against women's and gay and lesbian liberation movements. These movements had been extremely successful in changing attitudes, if not always actual policy, toward varying forms of sexual expression.

Between 1960 and 1980 the divorce rate climbed 200 percent, and by the early 1980s a majority of mothers were working outside the home (D'Emilio and Freedman, 332). Already in the 1960s these long-term trends were having visible consequences: the National Organization of Women was founded in 1966, and in 1969 the feminist Anne Koedt discussed the implications of William Masters and Virginia Johnson's research in a famous essay with radical consequences. The sexologists had demonstrated that female orgasm originated in the clitoris rather than in the vagina. In "The Myth of the Vaginal Orgasm," Koedt argued that such research proved that women's sexuality was constructed by men in their own interests. Psychoanalysts since Freud had insisted that normative female orgasm was vaginal in spite of scientific evidence to the contrary (not to mention women's experiences); women who had not experienced vaginal orgasm believed themselves to be deviant or unfulfilled.[31] Koedt questioned the naturalness of sexuality—and in particular of heterosexuality—by demonstrating that sexual pleasure could no longer be understood apart from the patriarchal social system that constructed it.[32] Moving beyond the insights of their interwar predecessors, radical feminists had thus come to recognize that sexual equality was itself a gendered concept.[33]

In June 1969 the gay rights movement was born in the three days of rioting that followed a police raid on the Stonewall Inn, a gay bar in New York's Greenwich Village. By the 1970s half of all states had eliminated sodomy statues from their penal codes, and in 1974 the American Psychiatric Association removed homosexuality from its list of mental disorders. As D'Emilio and Freedman have argued persuasively, the difference between the 1960s sexual revolution and the sexual "revolution" of the interwar years was that "the premium it placed upon fulfillment and pleasure compromised its ability to point sexual desire toward the institution of marriage" (325).

The resulting backlash against sexual liberalism manifested itself in several ways. Right-wing moralists found new popular support and mobilized their constituencies to place limits on abortion rights as well as on women's and gay and lesbian rights more generally. The 1976 Hyde Amendment prohibited the use of federal money to fund abortions. In the late 1970s conservatives sponsored several attacks on gay rights, among them, the singer Anita Bryant's 1977 "Save Our Children" campaign to repeal a gay rights ordinance in Dade County, Florida. New fears of contamination through sexual activity were fostered first by the spread of herpes and then by the "moral panic" that accompanied the discovery of the AIDS virus.[34] In the most direct statement of its agenda, "New Right" Christian conservatives attempted under President Ronald Reagan to resurrect the Family Protection Act, which would have denied federal funds to schools that "denigrate, diminish, or deny the role differences between the sexes" and present homosexuality "as an acceptable alternative life style" (quoted in D'Emilio and Freedman, 349).

The New Right also sought to increase censorship. It asserted that unrestrained sexual expression, especially pornography, caused violence, and violence against women in particular. Again, violence was conceived to have a privileged relationship to sexuality: violence was sexuality by another name. Although the effort to reinvigorate censorship on these grounds originated mainly in the right-wing moralism of the Citizens for Decency and the National Federation for Decency, only recently established by the Reverend Donald Wildmon, the emphasis on the link between sexuality and violence pervaded feminist, as well as some progressive nonfeminist, discussion of pornography.[35] The rhetoric of the right-wing backlash was predictable: it took up Comstock's old insistence that unbridled sexuality leads to violence, and it blamed permissiveness, the decline of the family, and women's and gay and lesbian emancipation for the rising consumption of pornography. Moreover, the New Right drew a causal relationship between pornography and violence and hoped to expand the powers of the federal government to restrict all kinds of explicit material, targeting sadomasochistic and homosexual pornography.

To conservatives' dismay, the congressional committee formed in 1970 to investigate the effects of pornography recommended by a vote of 12 to 5 to remove legal restrictions on adult use of pornographic material. The New Right's efforts would not be highly visible until the report of the 1986 Meese Commission (after Attorney General Edwin Meese), which could not prove a causal relationship between violence and sexual material but provided a spectacle of horrific, violence-laden images that were ostensibly mirrors of modern America's moral decay.[36]

My primary concern, however, is with the far less predictable feminist antipornography movement, whose members testified before the Meese Commission in support of censorship. That movement cannot properly be seen as a backlash. The antipornography movement followed the fragmentation of the women's liberation movement in the late 1970s. According to the historian Alice Echols, the interest in pornography was probably symptomatic of the movement's diversification and lack of a strong unifying issue to link women together, especially white women and women of color.[37] But the movement also provided advocates of women's civil rights with a means of defining pornography as discrimination without (at least theoretically) drawing on the traditional, patriarchal arguments of obscenity law advocates.

The contribution of antipornography feminists to the censorship debates must thus be understood within the context of left-wing challenges to the moral basis of right-wing arguments for antiob-scenity legislation. The main response to the New Right was represented by the ACLU's absolute defense of the First Amendment. Its argument was that acts and images are two different things, that "speech" is substantively different from action, and that there is thus no necessary relationship between the two. This position deals with the question of violence by denying any causal relationship between violent sexual practices (for example, rape) and violent sexual images, between violent acts and cultural representations of them.

Although the First Amendment still protects some allegedly obscene material, the "obscenity exception"—subjecting all contested material to the three criteria of scrutiny—is deemed "irrational" today by many free speech advocates. Explaining the obscenity exception as a concession to prudery and to religious and moral intolerance, they preach the virtues of a free society in which the liberal imagination has free rein. In an argument usually referred to metaphorically as a "slippery slope," they also insist that if some speech is censored, all speech is potentially endangered.

The anticensorship activist Marjorie Heins notes that there is simply no logical or historical rationale for obscenity legislation; she believes that all ideas are the product of free imaginations and should be accorded equal opportunity for expression (17). Heins presumes that in the "marketplace of ideas" there can be no normative standard of rationality since everyone's point of view must be considered equally valid, except for the legal standard of "direct incitement" (*Brandenberg v. Ohio* [1969]). The direct incitement ruling specifies that speech can be punished only when it incites individuals to reckless behavior (such as falsely shouting "Fire!" in a crowded theater); it thus pinpoints unreasonable speech and links it to tangible harm.

Although liberals conceive free speech as a right rather than a means of achieving social stability, Heins invokes (as Peckham did) the specter of antisocial behavior as a consequence of suppressing speech: "Blaming words or images is not merely an ineffective way to address social problems; it ignores both the cathartic and consciousness-raising functions of art. If feelings of anger, frustration, protest, or desperation can be expressed through the creative process, they're less likely to explode in anti-social behavior" (186). Moreover, Heins, who eloquently defends all speech, makes the familiar distinction between "genuine" creativity and implicitly less genuine imaginative expression (27), implying that some speech is in fact more deserving of protection than others, although she would never make legal policy on that basis. In other words, however valuable free speech is, its advocates do not consider speech and obscenity as historically produced categories that have changed over time; after all, the definition of "genuinely creative" work cannot be extricated from the social structures dominated by those deemed best suited to exercise social and moral judgment (mostly prominent white men).

The conceptual weaknesses of liberal ideology in its classical, pragmatic, and progressive variations have been explicated many times. They are just the sorts of weaknesses antipornography feminists exploit in their procensorship campaigns. Antipornography feminists also believe that freedom of expression guarantees social stability, but they challenge that guarantee by asking whose stability it protects and why. Where sexual liberals believe that the censorship of sexual expression leads to sadism (or "anti-social behavior"), antipornography feminists insist that censorship leads to sexual liberation and the end of sadism. Where free speech advocates see a clear distinction between words, images, and action, antipornography feminists see no distinction whatsoever. Where right-wing moralists cynically use increased violence against women as an argument for a return to patriarchally based protectionism, feminists see that violence as an instrument of patriarchy. Although the feminist position overlaps with others—they believe, with Legman, that seeing is doing and, with Edwin Meese, that pornography causes violence against women—they distinguish themselves by using gender as their principal category of analysis.

Many feminists, including Robin Morgan and Gloria Steinem, joined the struggle to mobilize the visceral, ambivalent, or negative responses of many women to pornography. The group Women Against Violence was founded in San Francisco in 1976, and related groups were formed in the late seventies in New York, Los Angeles, and Minneapolis. The first conference articulating a feminist position against pornography was held in San Francisco in November 1978, and the proceedings published as *Take Back the Night* (1980).[38]

In 1983 the prominent antipornography activists Catharine MacKinnon, a lawyer and legal scholar, and Andrea Dworkin, a writer, were invited by the Minneapolis City Council to draft an ordinance to regulate pornography in new terms. They redefined pornography as sex discrimination and aimed to censor all representations of women (and in another version, of men and transsexuals) that could be interpreted in any way as dehumanizing them. The ordinance language was so vague that nearly all forms of representation might have been subject to some sort of regulation—which was precisely their point: by targeting less explicitly pornographic forms of representation, MacKinnon and Dworkin wanted to demonstrate that unequal gender relations constructed and in turn were constructed by pornography. One of the most important works by the antipornography feminist Susanne Kappeler was entitled *The Pornography of Representation*.[39] This title indicates that all representation is pornographic: pornography cannot, as Linda Williams pointed out, be isolated in a pure state.

Ultimately, the antipornography ordinance sought to "desexualize" society in order to "resexualize" it, as one writer put it.[40] The ordinance passed the Minneapolis City Council but was vetoed by Mayor Donald Fraser. It was later passed by the conservative Indianapolis City Council. That vote was appealed, and the ordinance was struck down by successive courts whose decisions were confirmed when the Supreme Court refused to hear the case in 1986. The publicity surrounding the ordinance broadcast this feminist perspective on pornography to a national audience. To make their agenda more palatable to a wider public, traditional moralists replaced their emphasis on pornography's immorality with the ordinance's rhetoric of "violence against women." Finally, the antipornography movement initiated the most extensive and open discussion about female sexuality that had taken place within feminist ranks. It brought the issue to the fore with such urgency that even feminists who eventually opposed the antipornography forces were drawn into an important theoretical debate with serious legal and (other) social consequences.

An important conference at Barnard College in 1982 sought to encourage open discussion about sexuality among women. The proceedings were disrupted by antipornography feminists who used dubious tactics to silence women with whom they disagreed. The conference proceedings were published as *Pleasure and Danger* (1984); the editor, Carole Vance, urged women to "explore the ambiguous and complex relationship between sexual pleasure and danger in women's lives and in feminist theory" (3). Vance considered censorship merely another effort to sweep those complexities under the rug. Furthermore, the antipornography feminists' equation of sexuality and violence had the troubling effect of suggesting "that women are less sexually safe than ever and that discussions and explorations of pleasure are better deferred to a safer time" (6).

The feminist antipornography position can be understood in terms of a debate, once again, about the phantasmic image of the social body. Do antipornography feminists challenge the traditional premise that social stability is achieved through sexual purification—or more important, through purging femininity?

Antipornography Feminist Arguments

According to Catharine MacKinnon, the purpose of the antipornography movement is to give women words with which to articulate a reality of abuse and degradation that is now silenced in the name of free speech. Her writings are no paean to sexual liberation because, from her point of view, it is the ideologues of sexual liberation who have most effectively silenced women by defining liberation in terms of men's ability to use women sexually and to write about or film their fantasies as explicitly as they want. Moreover, those words and images are defined as "ideas" under the aegis of free speech. Our culture has become so saturated with pornography— the abuse of women protected as ideas—that men's sexual dominance over and dehumanization of women is reality: pornography constitutes social reality itself. Women are now victims of another "great war" in which their bodies, like those of soldiers, are reduced to machines; women, too, are duped into believing in the patriarchal system that destroys their humanity and are fed illusions of moral power and sublimity to compensate for their disempowerment. In a curious shift that has not been fully interrogated, heterosexual male desire is feminized—men vampirize and pollute women— and castigated for destroying the boundaried, integral selfhood proper to all human beings but denied to women by men.

Pornography thus constitutes a form of violence against women. Although MacKinnon's argument is close to Legman's, she departs from him in one important respect: for Legman, violence (sadism) is a displaced (and hence repressed) form of sexuality; for MacKinnon, sadistic violence is sexuality. Legman believed that readers of comic books were themselves repressed murderers; MacKinnon believes that consumers of pornography are sadists. Pornography, as she puts it, is "not only in the mind":

> As an initial matter, it should be observed that it is the pornography industry, not the ideas in the materials, that forces, threatens, blackmails, pressures, tricks, and cajoles women into sex for pictures. In pornography women are gang raped so they can be filmed. They are not gang raped by the idea of a gang rape. It is for pornography, and not by the ideas in it, that women are hurt and penetrated. . . . Only for pornography are women killed to make a sex movie, and it is not the idea of a sex killing that kills them. It is unnecessary to do any of these things to express, as ideas, the ideas pornography expresses. It is essential to do them to make pornography.[41]

MacKinnon's reasoning is indebted to speech act theory, first developed by the philosopher J. L. Austin in 1962 (MacKinnon, 1993, 21, 121n). She borrows his notion of performative speech to undo the opposition between speech and action (hence the title of her book, *Only Words*), although she never engages the various complicated theoretical positions of contemporary speech act theory.[42]

Even on her own terms, MacKinnon leaves a very important question unresolved. What exactly does it mean to do something "for" pornography? She hints at a response: to be for pornography is to be for "erections that support aggression against women in particular" and to support behavior to which men become "sexually habituated" through "primitive conditioning" by words and pictures (1993, 16). Pornography is uncontrollable, mostly male sexual behavior that is continuous with thought: having sex is not antithetical to thinking but "*is* thinking" (1993, 17).

Feminist theorists and others have commented on the globalizing reasoning that pervades MacKinnon's writing: pornography is a sort of transcendental principle, a bottom line, as it were, that both explains and expresses social inequity.[43] MacKinnon never explains how pornography constitutes our thinking or "reality," how it constitutes gender inequity; it just does. The following passage is representative of this elision: "Gender is sexual. Pornography constitutes the meaning of that sexuality. Men treat women as whom they see women as being. Pornography constructs who that is. Men's power over women means that the way men see women defines who women can be. Pornography is that way."[44]

MacKinnon cannot define the relationship between gender inequality and pornography except tautologically. Consequently, because of her refusal to explain how one constitutes the other, the relationship between them cannot be accounted for except as one that has always been "that way." She characterizes gender relations exclusively in binary terms that appear to be universal and inescapable: dominance/submission, subject/object, male/female. This tendency to turn women's sexuality solely into a site of danger, to repeat Carole Vance, has been the most frequent subject of dissenting feminists' criticism. The dichotomy between men and women is certainly central to the antipornography feminist position. However, their construction of male sexuality is far more complicated than they or their critics suggest.

Antipornography Feminism and Male Sexuality

The antipornography feminists' conception of male sexuality is more paradoxical than monolithic or uni-directional. First, pornography expresses men's lack of self-control. But as a product of the smooth operations of capitalism, pornography also represents social control. This paradox of a controlled loss of control plays out as the male's struggle to consolidate himself through the total control of women—he makes women extensions of his own sexual needs and so silences theirs. Pornography is a tool of social control and bolsters capitalist production in the interests of men.[45] To be "for" pornography is to be "for" the total control of men over women.

At the same time, to be for pornography is to celebrate men's lack of self-restraint, to encourage them to want and need greater and riskier taboos. To be for pornography is to encourage addictive behavior that men cannot stop, to encourage them, to use the liberals' metaphor, to descend down a slippery slope whose summit and base are both pornography itself. According to the antipornography activist Corrine Sweet, pornography is an addiction like any other: it is no different from addictions to sugar, cocaine, caffeine, masturbation, and gambling and is a form of self-abuse (182, 188–93). Pornography addicts move from soft porn to hard porn and finally to doing what they see or read. Pornography is contagious, poisonous, and polluting: one critic urges us to "de-toxify" society and ourselves; another draws an analogy between environmental pollution and pornography; yet another writes that "once you have been exposed to pornography and its users you are infected for life."[46]

Pornography is the absolute loss of control expressed as absolute control. Or to put it another way, men's lack of sexual self-control is continuous with total social control. Men's self-abuse leads to their need to abuse and thus control women. The (contested) cliché that abuse begets abuse does not explain how men can exercise absolute hegemony and be absolutely lacking in the self-restraint necessary for orderly, dispassionate profit-making. Greedy people, after all, must be calculating and patient. It hardly bears repeating that in morality tales those who are too greedy, who are impatient, lose in the end: they are not successful capitalists. They do not become sex industry magnates, who think of themselves (as do many sex workers) as competent, calculating businesspeople.

Antipornography feminists claim that pornography expresses the impact of socioeconomic structures on gender, and yet their arguments beg the question about the relationship between those structures and individual men: "Acknowledging pornography is addictive does not let men off the hook" (Sweet, 199). Consumers of pornography are pawns of capitalism and patriarchy, but they are also the beneficiaries of these social systems. We must look beyond the obvious inadequacies of this argument to understand why it makes sense to the feminists who espouse it.

In the antipornography view, men who have not learned to control their addiction to pornography act it out under cover of or in the name of the law, specifically the First Amendment. Weak, unrestrained men masquerade as heroes, champions of free speech; much like the white male suburbanite, the new corrupter is, to quote Legman again, "too unvirile to throw off fear, and kill as [a] criminal. Instead, unseen and unsuspected in some corner, they put on a black mask, a sheriff's badge . . . and do all their killing on the side of the law" (43). Of course, antipornography feminists would never use this language, but its logic is evident in their desire to restore men (and women) to wholeness, to relieve them of their sexual addictions. We are told again and again that the pornography consumer is a fearful man, afraid he is not virile enough, emotionally repressed, and often sexually abused. Pornography—abuse carried out as free speech, violence done in the name of the law—gives such men the illusion of self-control. If we were to censor pornography, we would replace this personally and socially destructive illusion of self-control with real, affirming self-control (Sweet, 179–200).

The analogy between the pathetic (implicitly homosexual) fascist and the pathetic pornography consumer—both seek absolute control because of their real lack of self-control—is implied in the title of an essay, "Working in the Ministry of Truth," that appeared in a recent collection of (mostly recycled) antipornography essays (Moorcock, 536–52). The Orwellian allusion links the sex industry to the totalitarian mind control exercised by fascists who, we know from Adorno and Legman, are not real men. Like fascists, consumers of pornography (unlike enlightened men who join the antipornography movement and own up to their addictive behavior) need to dehumanize others (primarily women) in order to consolidate their own sense of self. Thus, pornography is evidence less of men's self-possession than of their pathological ("conditioned") lack of boundaries expressed and experienced as omnipotence: "They'll always reinterpret the behavior of the victim. They will say the victim encouraged them, or seduced them, or asked for it, or wanted it, or enjoyed it. And if the victim survives the abuse they will interpret that to mean they were in no way harmed by it."[47]

Restoring Sexual Subjectivity

Although antipornography discourse now focuses more on women's "addiction" to pornography, and although its rhetoric appears to explain women's oppression, its central concern nevertheless remains men's emptiness and the consequences of men's insatiability. Pornography constructs men's emptiness as plenitude, their self-division as self-constitution. MacKinnon most explicitly describes this paradoxical relationship between male sexuality and selfhood: "[Pornography] creates an accessible sexual object, the possession and consumption of which is male sexuality, to be possessed and consumed as which is female sexuality. This is not because pornography depicts objectified sex, but because it creates the experience of a sexuality which is itself objectified" (1989, 140–41). In creating the experience of an objectified sexuality, pornography constitutes and consolidates male sexuality as an illusory form of self-possession.

To restore both men's and women's selfhood, we must therefore eliminate pornography. But to the extent that MacKinnon conceives pornography as denying women's and producing men's (illusory) selfhood, *selfhood can be restored, paradoxically, only if it is severed from sexuality.* The only way to restore integral selves (those not suffering from illusory compensation for their real self-division, those not "addicted" to pornography's illusion of self-consolidation) is to draw an absolute line between sexuality and the self. This goes for both women and men, but its consequences and burden are especially devastating for women. Since MacKinnon implicitly argues that women can be selves only to the extent that they have no sexuality, women's liberation, including women's sexual freedom, depends on the repudiation of sexuality.[48]

Again and again, antipornography feminists reiterate the idea that for women sexuality and selfhood are entirely incompatible in our culture. MacKinnon invokes Ti-Grace Atkinson's comment, "I do not know any feminist worthy of that name, who, if forced to choose between freedom and sex, would choose sex. She'd choose freedom every time" (1989, 154). But perhaps the most forceful expression of the sundering of freedom from sexuality is Andrea Dworkin's interpretation of Joan of Arc. In her homage to the woman warrior, Dworkin equates integral subjectivity with manliness, which can be achieved only through the repudiation of sexuality: "She incarnated virtue in its original meaning: strength or manliness. Her virginity was an essential element of her virility, her autonomy, her rebellious and intransigent self-definition. Her virginity was a radical renunciation of a civil worthlessness rooted in real sexual practice."[49] Women cannot be strong and sexually active at the same time: to have a self-definition, women must renounce sexuality—because sexuality in our culture is a form of degradation for women. Joan of Arc is glorious because she was armored literally and figuratively against corporeal violation. Joan of Arc is not the feminized, duped, and polluted combat veteran of the Great War, but the pure woman warrior whose warrior status is dependent on her purity—that is to say, her virility.

Moreover, this paradox whereby selfhood can be achieved only through the repudiation of sexuality is subtended by another paradox: women can become sexual agents only to the extent that they recognize themselves as objects. MacKinnon claims that women's sexuality is constituted as objectified sexuality. Yet her followers argue implicitly that women become sexual addicts and users of pornography only if they are abused or brainwashed. But if women are constituted as and can only experience themselves as sexual objects, from what vantage point might they recognize their objectification? And, if women experience themselves as objects, why would they have to be abused ir brainwashed to enjoy pornography, which represents who women think they are?

This suggests that antipornography feminists have an operative, normative concept of female sexuality in spite of their claims that all sexuality is socially constructed. One does not have to look hard to find it: women prefer "erotica" to pornography; women prefer the context of a relationship for sexual expression and repudiate sex for the sake of sex (Baker, 231).[50] How can women be denied sexual agency altogether but also recognize that their agency has been denied them? From what subject position do women speak?

In the antipornography feminists' universe, women can achieve subject status only if they refashion themselves after a self forever lost, after the integral, whole self the sexual revolutionaries sought to restore. This liberal, enlightened, boundaried self is the only historical precedent for MacKinnon's concept of the ideal human relationship and ideal human sexuality. The antipornography feminist movement, for all its radicalism, essentially works with a normative, idealized, and phantasmic image of the contained and controlled human body. These feminists seek to restore the human body to its "original" unified state, to make its exterior form coextensive with its interior substance, by purging it of its femininity and, more specifically, by displacing the cultural narrative about the dangers of femininity onto male heterosexuality: now women are uncontaminated and integral and men are fragmented and diseased. Male heterosexuality is vampiric: it invades and drains women's bodies and takes tantalizing and seductive forms that prove irresistible and yet life-destroying. In short, antipornography feminists apparently seek to liberate female sexuality by defending it from femininity, and to liberate womanhood in order to purify it of the fluidity and contamination historically associated with female sexuality.

Replication and Transformation

On the other hand, this desexualization of women's bodies in the name of assigning them respectability is no simple return to Victorianism. It is true, as I have already argued, that MacKinnon's and Dworkin's ideas have replicated and legitimated the current status of lesbians and gay men (and less directly, African Americans) as repositories of contaminated and contaminating femininity. After Canadian obscenity law was amended to include MacKinnon's definition of "harm against women," the first publication to be prosecuted was a lesbian erotic (and sadomasochistic) magazine, *Bad Attitude*.

In the United States, as I mentioned earlier, religious fundamentalists seized on the language of "harm against women" to legitimate obscenity charges against the African American rappers Two Live Crew. MacKinnon and Dworkin were silent about the unsuccessful prosecution of a Cincinnati museum director who chose to exhibit the photographs of the gay male sadomasochist Robert Mapplethorpe, and they maintained their silence when four artists, three of whom were lesbian or gay men, were denied funding from the National Endowment for the Arts. This silence, which is hard to interpret, gives the impression of complicity. By theorizing about pornography in a vacuum, antipornography feminists appear to endorse the repression of traditionally excluded social groups. Do they believe that the current targeting of sadomasochists—of whom they do not approve no matter what their sexual orientation—is distinct from a broader conservative agenda to target all nonconformists, especially sexual dissidents? As I mentioned earlier, Senator Jesse Helms's recent obscenity amendment makes evident the New Right's efforts to use censorship laws to focus explicitly on sadomasochism and homosexuality.

Why then, if the ordinance has such reactionary effects, is it not simply a return to Victorian mores? MacKinnon, Dworkin, and their followers never deny women's sexuality or associate it explicitly with contamination; instead, as we have seen, all questions about the meaning of female sexuality are deferred by the contradiction in their argument: women's sexuality is at once socially constructed by patriarchy and essentially more egalitarian than men's. That is, women's egalitarian sexuality is repressed by patriarchal sexual relations even as their sexuality is constituted in and through those relations.

In spite of their apparent insistence on an egalitarian concept of female sexuality, antipornography feminists in effect treat that concept the way revolutionaries too often treat the revolution: as an event "to come," in the future, deferred. That is why, we recall, Joan Hoff insists that we must "desexualize" society in order to resexualize it: in other words, no women can have the subject status of which feminists dream until the revolution is over. The most theoretically sophisticated antipornography feminists, including MacKinnon, conclude that women are merely extensions of men's fantasies. In other words, it is men and not women who are unrestrained, lacking, and fragmented, since women do not exist except as men's self-projections. Most of the talk about women's inherent egalitarianism is self-consciously utopian. It does not matter if it is true or not. The real focus of antipornography feminism is not women's sexuality but men's.

Unlike the Victorians, then, antipornography feminists believe the very idea of sexuality, pure or impure, is a socially constructed male fantasy, and they do not seek to empower women by heralding them as emblems of moral self-restraint (although, in contradiction with their own pronouncements, they often idealize an inherently egalitarian, impermeable female sexuality). On the one hand, they presume that modern sexuality has no natural referent—that it is the reflection and production of historically specific, fragmented male selves. This presumption is in keeping with the erosion of the natural foundations of gender difference since the nineteenth-century. On the other hand, antipornography feminists also seek to reinvent sexual relations in new terms by restoring integrated, impermeable bodies. Although they do not therefore wish to restore conventional gender boundaries—as did male elites since the turn of the century—they do sustain the paradox whereby "healthy" sexuality can be realized only through the desexualizing of the self.

Thus antipornography feminists contribute to the erosion of normative masculinity and femininity—in their vision, the two are indistinct—*and* they resurrect a vision of men and women unsullied by sexuality. In spite of their desire to liberate women from patriarchal constraints, this vision is itself inextricable from the normative and gendered, male model of selfhood that has historically associated women, gay men and lesbians, and people of color with sexuality and denied them rights on that basis.

Some of the political uses to which antipornography feminism has been put demonstrates that the regulation of sexuality will continue to target these groups.[51] Sexual regulation remains an effort to control the putatively disruptive effects of femininity and all that it stands for: atavism, fluidity, contagion, loss of self-control.

Conclusion

In this book I have argued that since the midnineteenth century the regulation and reconstruction of gender boundaries have marked the dialectical points of departure for new and increasingly fluid constructions of sexuality—always in formation, never boundaried. Indeed, a more mutable model of sexuality has begun to take shape as an alternative to conventional models, and that fact may partly explain the current struggle over questions of sexual and gender identity between the Left and the Right, and especially within the American Left. Recall the deep divisions antipornography feminists produced within the feminist movement after the early 1980s; within the gay rights movement, those who celebrate lesbian or gay identity as a form of stable sexuality are often at odds with those who propound the more fluid model of "queer"—fluid, changing, and unstable—sexuality.

Historians have only recently begun to tell different stories about the emergence of new sorts of sexual and gender identities. In this book I have attempted to synthesize these stories. In both the primary and secondary literature I have investigated, modern Western sexuality is constituted through efforts, diverse and systematic, informal and formal, to regulate the relationship between gender and the self in historically specific terms. But the history of sexuality also demonstrates that, however successful those efforts, they can never fully capture the shifting meanings of gender, sexuality, and selfhood.

Chronology

1864–1869 Britain passes the Contagious Diseases Acts.

1868 Dr. Karoly Maria Benkert coins the word *homosexuality*.

1871 The Paris Commune uprising takes place. Germany begins regulating prostitution.

1873 The Comstock Law is passed, making it a crime to send "obscene matter" through the U.S. Postal Service.

1877 Annie Besant and Charles Bradlaugh are tried in London for distributing birth control literature.

1883 The term "eugenics" is invented in England by Francis Galton.

1884 French divorce law reforms are passed.

1885 Britain passes the Criminal Amendment Act criminalizing male homosexual acts and raising the age of consent for girls from 12 to 16.

1886 Richard von Krafft-Ebing publishes *Psychopathia Sexualis*. Contagious Diseases Acts are repealed in England.

1891 Germany passes protective legislation limiting women's work and mandating maternity leave.

1894   Edward Carpenter publishes *Homogenic Love in a Free Society*.

1896   Paul Robin founds the French Neo-Malthusian League.

1897   Magnus Hirschfeld and others form the first homosexual rights organization, the Scientific-Humanitarian Committee.

1897–1910   Havelock Ellis publishes *Studies in the Psychology of Sex*.

1903   Women's Social and Political Union founded in England.

1904   First International Women's Suffrage Alliance meets in Berlin.

1905   Freud publishes *Three Essays on the Theory of Sexuality*. Helene Stöcker establishes the League for the Protection of Maternity and Sexual Reform in Germany. "Sex chromosomes" are discovered.

1908   Magnus Hirschfeld begins publication of the *Journal of Sexology*.

1914   World War I begins.

1917   Russian Revolution begins. French women are granted primary guardianship of their children.

1918   World War I ends. British women win limited suffrage.

1919   German women win suffrage.

1920   U.S. women win suffrage. French law makes distribution of birth control information a crime and abortion a capital crime. Marie Stopes publishes *Married Love*.

1921   First International Congress for Sexual Reform is held in Berlin.

1929   Britain passes the Infant Life Act.

1933   Hitler becomes chancellor of Germany.

1934   James Joyce's *Ulysses* is tried in the United States and found to be nonpornographic.

1938   Britain permits abortion to protect mothers from "physical or emotional distress." Virginia Woolf publishes *Three Guineas*.

1939   World War II begins.

1944   French women win suffrage.

1945   World War II ends. Italian women win suffrage.

1948   Alfred Kinsey's study of male sexuality is published.

1950   A U.S. congressional committee issues its report on homosexuals in the government.

1952   "Homosexual panic" is codified as a psychological disorder in the *Diagnostic and Statistical Manual of the Psychiatric Profession*.

1953   Alfred Kinsey's study of female sexuality is published. President Eisenhower issues an executive order banning gay men and lesbians from federal employment.

1957   Obscenity is redefined in *Roth v. the United States*.

1966   The National Organization of Women is founded.

1967   Sale of contraceptives is legalized in France. Abortion is legalized in Britain.

1969   The gay rights movement begins with the Stonewall Inn uprising. Anne Koedt publishes "The Myth of the Vaginal Orgasm."

1970   A U.S. congressional committee votes to remove legal restrictions on the use of pornography by consenting adults.

1973   *Miller v. California* affirms the criteria for determining obscenity. Abortion is legalized in the United States. The Boston Women's Health Collective publishes *Our Bodies, Our Selves*.

1974   The American Psychiatric Association removes homosexuality from its list of mental disorders.

1975   Abortion is legalized in France.

1976   The Hyde Amendment prohibiting federal funding of abortion is passed. Michel Foucault publishes *The*

History of Sexuality. Women Against Violence is founded in San Francisco.

1978   The first feminist antipornography conference is held in San Francisco.

1982   Conference on "Towards a Politics of Women's Sexuality" at Barnard College.

1983   Catharine MacKinnon and Andrea Dworkin draft an antipornography ordinance for the Minneapolis City Council.

1985   The MacKinnon-Dworkin ordinance is found unconstitutional by a Federal Court. The Supreme Court denies *certiorati*.

1986   The Meese Commission presents its report on pornography.

1988   The British Parliament passes Section 28 to prohibit local authorities from "intentionally promoting homosexuality."

Notes and References

INTRODUCTION

1. Jeffrey Weeks, *Sexuality* (London: Routledge, 1989), 21.

2. Paul Robinson, *The Modernization of Sex: Havelock Ellis, Alfred Kinsey, William Masters, and Virginia Johnson* (Ithaca, N.Y.: Cornell University Press, 1989), 178; hereafter cited in text.

3. Michel Foucault, *The History of Sexuality*, vol. 1 (New York: Vintage, 1980); hereafter cited in text.

4. According to the *Oxford English Dictionary*, *sexuality* was first used in England in 1879 in a gynecological textbook to refer to sex as an instinct independent of the woman's anatomy. See Arnold Davidson, "Sex and the Emergence of Sexuality," *Critical Inquiry* 14, (Autumn, 1987): 23.

5. Richard von Krafft-Ebing, *Psychopathia Sexualis*, trans. Harry E. Wedeck (New York: Putnam, 1965).

6. The word *heterosexual* was also invented at this time. First used in English in 1892, the word appeared in German perhaps as early as 1868 but was not printed in that language until 1880. Yet *heterosexual* still had a variety of meanings, including the meaning we now attribute to *bisexual*. David Halperin notes that the man who coined the term *homosexual* opposed it to *normalsexual*. In his 1905 work on Berlin homosexuals, Magnus Hirschfeld also used the term *normalsexual*. The word *homosexual* was first coined in 1868 in the context of efforts to repeal paragraph 175 of the Prussian penal code, which criminalized sodomy (see chapter 2). David Halperin, *One Hundred Years of Homosexuality and*

Other Essays on Greek Love (New York: Routledge, 1990), 158–59, 17n; Jonathan N. Katz, *The Gay/Lesbian Almanac* (New York: Harper & Row, 1983), 1476–50–51.

7. Much of the revisionist criticism of Victorian sexuality redefines our vision of Victorians as sexually repressed by demonstrating that certain clichés about Victorian society are not borne out by the evidence. Books by Steven Marcus, Martha Vicinus, Peter Gay, Carl Degler, and Carroll Smith-Rosenberg (see Bibliography), among others, have been extremely important in this regard, in spite of their interpretative differences. For a recent and compelling critique of this work, see Steven Seidman, "The Power of Desire and the Danger of Pleasure: Victorian Sexuality Reconsidered," *Journal of Social History* Vol. 24, 1 (1990): 47–67. The most recent of these revisionist arguments is Michael Mason, *The Making of Victorian Sexuality* (Oxford: Oxford University Press, 1994); hereafter cited in text. In contrast to the other scholars just mentioned, Mason is almost entirely uninformed by more recent historical surveys, seems impervious to gender as a category of analysis, and in my view, completely misreads Foucault (172–73). Moreover, he discusses the "making" of Victorian sexuality almost exclusively in demographic terms.

8. Because there is so little secondary source material, Russia and Eastern Europe cannot be coherently synthesized into this account. One recent work on Imperial Russia that does grapple with some of the main issues considered in this book is Laura Engelstein, *The Keys to Happiness: Sex and the Search for Modernity in Fin-de-Siècle Russia* (Ithaca, N.Y.: Cornell University Press, 1992). There is also a vast literature on the social history of Russian women that for the most part does not engage the history of sexuality.

It is of course impossible to cover all the dimensions of the history of sexuality or to account for why it has evolved differently in different national cultures. I have drawn mostly on secondary source material concerning North America, Britain, France, and Germany in order to make a more general argument.

CHAPTER 1

1. See Lesley A. Hall, "Forbidden by God, Despised by Men: Masturbation, Medical Warnings, Moral Panic, and Manhood in Great Britain," and John D. Fout, "Sexual Politics in Wilhelmine Germany: The Male Gender Crisis, Moral Purity, and Homophobia," both in *Forbidden History: The State, Society, and the Regulation of Sexuality in Modern Europe*, ed. John C. Fout (Chicago: University of Chicago Press, 1992), 293–316; 259–92; both hereafter cited in text.

2. Thomas Laqueur, *Making Sex: Body and Gender from the Greeks to Freud* (Cambridge, Mass.: Harvard University Press, 1990); hereafter cited in text.

3. Barbara Meil Hobson, *Uneasy Virtue: The Politics of Prostitution and the American Reform Tradition* (Chicago: University of Chicago Press, 1990), 191; hereafter cited in text. On the links between unrestrained female sexuality and African women's sexuality, see Sander L. Gilman, *Difference and Pathology: Stereotypes of Sexuality, Race, and Madness* (Ithaca, N.Y.: Cornell University Press, 1985), 76–108.

4. Alexandre Parent-Duchâtelet, *De la prostitution dans la ville de Paris, considérée sous le rapport de l'hygiène publique, de la morale et de l'administration*, Paris, 1836.

5. Londa L. Schiebinger, "Skeletons in the Closet: The First Illustrations of the Female Skeleton in Eighteenth-Century Anatomy," in *The Making of the Modern Body: Sexuality and Society in the Nineteenth Century*, ed. Catherine Gallagher and Thomas Laqueur (Berkeley: University of California Press, 1987), 42–82.

6. Edmund Burke, *Reflections on the Revolution in France* [1790], ed. Conor Cruise O'Brien (New York: Penguin, 1982), 165; Maxime Du Camp, *Les Convulsions de Paris* (Paris: Hachette, 1879), 122.

7. For excellent discussions of both Zola and Du Camp, see Susanna Barrows, *Distorting Mirrors: Visions of the Crowd in Late Nineteenth-Century France* (New Haven: Yale University Press, 1981); and Janet Beizer, *Ventriloquized Bodies: Narratives of Hysteria in Nineteenth-Century France* (Ithaca, N.Y.: Cornell University Press, 1993).

8. Married, middle-class, white women were also sexual property, but they were presumed to be sexually passive; their status *as* property must be differentiated from black women's not only in terms of their minimal legal rights but in terms of the cultural value accorded their sexuality.

9. Sander Gilman, *Difference and Pathology: Stereotypes of Sexuality, Race, and Madness* (Ithaca: Cornell University Press, 1985), 83.

10. Karin J. Jusek, "Sexual Morality and the Meaning of Prostitution in Fin-de-Siècle Vienna," in *From Sappho to De Sade: Moments in the History of Sexuality*, ed. Jan Bremmer (New York: Routledge, 1989), 126; hereafter cited in text.

11. The consequences of ignoring the paradoxical status of Victorian womanhood are best illustrated in Michael Mason's recent book. Asserting that a doctor making "the connection between menstruation and [female animals] being in heat at all is actually something of a tribute to his sense of a woman's libido," Mason proposes that we view this fact—which is clear evidence of the hardly flattering analogy Victorian doctors drew between women and animals—as an important

corrective to other doctors' view that "women are less urgent in their sexuality" (196).

12. William Acton, *The Function and Disorders of the Reproductive Organs in Youth, Adult Age, and Advanced Life, Considered in Their Physiological, Social, and Psychological Relations* (London: John Churchill, 1857), 119.

13. In England especially, there was a fledgling "free love" movement in the 1890s (including the sexual reformers Edward Carpenter and Grant Allen), but its views were not widely considered until after 1900, particularly after the Great War.

14. See also William Greenslade, *Degeneration, Culture and the Novel, 1880–1940* (Cambridge: Cambridge University Press, 1994), 182–83. The voluminous literature on Empire and sexuality makes the same general argument with many nuances.

15. Andreas Huyssen, *After the Great Divide: Modernism, Mass Culture, Postmodernism* (Bloomington: Indiana University Press, 1986), 55.

16. Otto Weininger, *Sex and Character* (London: Heinemann, 1910).

17. See Alain Corbin, "Commercial Sexuality in Nineteenth-century France: A System of Images and Regulations," in Gallagher and Laqueur, *Making of the Modern Body*, 209–219; and Judith Walkowitz, *City of Dreadful Delight: Narratives of Sexual Danger in Late-Victorian London* (Chicago: University of Chicago Press, 1992); hereafter cited in text.

18. Judith Walkowitz, *Prostitution and Victorian Society: Women, Class, and the State* (Cambridge: Cambridge University Press, 1980), hereafter cited in text; Angus McLaren, *A Prescription for Murder: The Victorian Serial Killings of Dr. Thomas Neill Cream* (Chicago: University of Chicago Press, 1993).

19. See Carroll Smith-Rosenberg, *Disorderly Conduct: Visions of Gender in Victorian America* (Oxford: Oxford University Press, 1985), 220–21; hereafter cited in text.

20. Quoted in Walter Kendrick, *The Secret Museum: Pornography in Modern Culture* (New York: Viking Penguin, 1987), 121. Kendrick also writes about Flaubert's and Baudelaire's trials in detail (95–124). There is a voluminous literature on these trials.

21. The first U.S. law against obscenity was passed in 1842 and was directed against imported pictures. The law was strengthened in 1857 to include books. See David Loth, *The Erotic Motive in Literature* (New York: Dorset Press, 1961), 142; hereafter cited in text.

22. For an account of this scandal, see Isabelle Hull, *The Entourage of Kaiser Wilhelm II, 1888–1918* (Cambridge: Cambridge University Press, 1982). Hereafter cited in text.

23. Max Nordau, *Degeneration* (New York: Appleton, 1895), 169.

24. Achille Segard, *Les Volupteux et les hommes d'action* (Paris: Société d'éditions littéraires et artistiques, 1900), 97–100.

25. Arnold Davidson, "Closing up the Corpses: Diseases of Sexuality and the Emergence of the Psychiatric Style of Reasoning," in *Meaning and Method: Essays in Honor of Hilary Putnam*, ed. George Boolos (Cambridge: Cambridge University Press, 1990), 314; hereafter cited in text.

26. Leo Taxil (pseudonym of Gabriel Jogand-Pagès), *La Prostitution contemporaine, étude d'une question sociale* (Paris: Librarie Populaire, 1884), 287–89.

27. Dr. G. St. Paul, *Thèmes psychologiques: Invertis et homosexuels* [1897], 3d ed. (Paris: Vigot Frères, 1930), 11. The unconscious irony of this statement is worth noting: the "private" selves of male homosexuals were compromised by sexual acts they often if not always performed in public—in a visible yet "hidden" or disreputable urban locale where young and poor male prostitutes made themselves available.

CHAPTER 2

1. Gert Hekma, "A History of Sexology: Social and Historical Aspects of Sexuality," in Bremmer, *From Sappho to De Sade*, 176–77; hereafter cited in text.

2. Joanny Roux, *Psychologie de l'instinct sexuel* (Paris: J. B. Ballière et Fils, 1899), 23–25.

3. Quoted in Paul Chavigny, *Psychologie de l'hygiène* (Paris: Flammarion, 1921), 51.

4. Sigmund Freud, *Three Essays on the Theory of Sexuality*, trans. James Strachey (New York: Basic Books, 1975), 34.

5. Like Ann-Louise Shapiro, one could also use female criminality more generally to demonstrate how narratives about women "lost [their] ability to contain the embedded contradictions about woman's nature and woman's place"—perhaps because female criminality was so inextricable from narratives about female sexuality. My discussion is quite similarly structured, though I use homosexuality to cast the argument in the broadest terms possible. See Ann-Louise Shapiro, "Love Stories: Female Crimes of Passion in Fin-de-Siècle Paris," *differences: A Journal of Feminist Cultural Studies"* 3, no. 3 (1991): 47.

6. Ulrichs also coined the term "Uranism" to refer to male homosexuals. Used until the Great War, the term refers to Aphrodita Urania, the patroness of men who love men in Plato's *Symposium*. See James D. Steakley, *The Homosexual Rights Movement in Germany* (Salem, Mass.: Ayer Co., 1982), 8.

7. Karl Westphal, "Die conträre Sexualempfindung," *Archiv für Psychiatrie und Nervenkrankheiten* 2:1 (August 1869), 73–108.

8. Henry Havelock Ellis, *Sexual Inversion*, in *Studies in the Psychology of Sex*, vol. 1 (New York: Random House, 1905), esp. 82–84; hereafter cited in text.

9. The German term *Der Eigene* implies both otherness (in the sense of something strange) and individual autonomy, thus making it possible in this context to give otherness a positive valence. George Mosse, *Nationalism and Sexuality: Respectability and Abnormal Sexuality in Modern Europe* (New York: Fertig, 1985), 42–43. Hereafter cited in text.

10. Quoted in Lillian Faderman and Brigitte Eriksson, *Lesbians in Germany: 1890s–1920s* (Tallahassee: Naiad Press, 1990), xiv; hereafter cited in text.

11. Quoted in George Chauncey, Jr., "From Sexual Inversion to Homosexuality: Medicine and the Changing Conceptualization of Female Deviance," *Salmagundi* 58–59 (Fall–Winter 1983): 119.

12. Magnus Hirschfeld, *Berlins Dritte Geschlecht, Schwule und Lesben um 1900* [1905] (reprint, Berlin: Verlag Rosa Winkel, 1991).

13. In France, for example, the word *sexuality* did not appear in dictionaries in its modern sense—to describe a person's character as well as his or her anatomical development—until 1924, in reference to Freud's own work (*Three Essays*). See Robert Nye, *Masculinity and Male Codes of Honor in Modern France* (Oxford: Oxford University Press, 1993), 117; hereafter cited in text.

14. See the works of Alan Berube, John D'Emilio, Lillian Faderman, and Jeffrey Weeks, as well as *Hidden from History*, edited by Martin Duberman, Martha Vicinus, and George Chauncey, Jr., all listed in the Bibliography.

15. Recent works by Terry Castle, Judith Butler, Joan Nestle, and others are attempts to raise the question of lesbian sexuality. Most of these authors are not historians. See Judith Butler, "The Lesbian Phallus and the Morphological Imaginary," *differences: A Journal of Feminist Cultural Studies* 2, no. 2 (1990): 133–71; Terry Castle, *The Apparitional Lesbian: Female Homosexuality in Modern Culture* (New York: Columbia University Press, 1993); Elizabeth Grosz, "Lesbian Fetishism" *differences: A Journal of Feminist Cultural Studies* 3, no. 2 (1991): 39–54; Elizabeth Lapovsky Kennedy and Madeline B. Davis, *Boots of Leather, Slippers of Gold: The History of a Lesbian Community* (New York: Routledge, 1993); and Joan Nestle, *A Restricted Country* (Ithaca, N.Y.: Firebrand Books, 1987).

16. Renée Vivien, *Une Femme m'apparut* (Paris: Desforges, 1977), 36–41. Since Faderman's important work has a tendency to downplay women's same-sex behavior in favor of "spiritual" relationships, these translations must be used with circumspection. I did not have access to the original sources.

17. Dr. L. Thoinot, *Attentat aux moeurs et perversions du sens génital* (Paris: Octave Doin, 1898), 318; hereafter cited in text.

18. It is no surprise that the infamous 1832 French pornographic novel *Gamiani*, rumored to have been written by Alfred de Musset as revenge against George Sand, mirrors precisely these views. In it, a famous lesbian countess and her lover take poison during lovemaking so they might experience orgasm and death simultaneously. *Gamiani, ou, Deux nuits d'excès* (Paris: l'Or du Temps, 1970).

19. Dr. Caufeynon [pseudonym of Jean Fauconney], *Les Vices féminins* (Paris: Librarie Artistique, 1923), 41–42.

20. See Nicole Albert, "Sappho Mythified, Sappho Mystified, or the Metamorphoses of Sappho in Fin-de-Siècle France," in *Gay Studies from the French Cultures: Voices from France, Belgium, Brazil, Canada, and the Netherlands*, ed. Rommel Mendès-Leite and Pierre Olivier de Busscher (New York: Haworth Press, 1993), 87–104. The word *Sapho* was associated with the "morals attributed to Sappho" rather than with sexual practices in the 1842 *Grand Larousse encyclopédique du XIXème siècle*. See Albert, "Sappho Mythified," 93; Algernon Charles Swinburne, *Lesbia Brandon* (London: Falcon Press, 1952); Charles Baudelaire, *"Femmes damnées"* (Delphine et Hippolyte) and *"Lesbos,"* in *Les Fleurs du mal* (Paris: Gallimard, 1972), 149–50, 176–82. For a synthesis of the myriad works on lesbianism in the late nineteenth century, see Nicole Albert, "Lesbos et la décadence," *Diplôme d'études approfondies* Paris IV, 1986. The article cited above is a revised and translated excerpt from this text.

21. "Dr. Samuel," *La Flagellation dans les maisons de tolérance* (Paris: Maurice Wandnoël, n.d.), 32–33.

22. The fact that lesbians were rarely persecuted does not contradict this argument: legislators claimed that persecuting lesbianism would give women ideas about it they may not already have had.

CHAPTER 3

1. Emmanuel Berl, *The Nature of Love* (New York, 1924), 15.

2. Karl Toepfer, "Nudity and Modernity in German Dance, 1910–1930," *Journal of the History of Sexuality* 1 (1992): 101; hereafter cited in text. Toepfer's article gives an overview—in the context of German dance—of the reconstruction of heterosexuality and its relation, at least implicitly, to the postwar self.

3. Because war was still the ultimate test of real citizenship and women were excluded from combat, they could still technically be excluded from full political rights. The notion that self-sacrifice for one's country constitutes the "true" test of loyalty is still with us and still

works against women (and men who have not fought in combat) who seek high political office.

4. Quoted in Kevin White, *The First Sexual Revolution: The Emergence of Male Heterosexuality in Modern America* (New York: New York University Press, 1993), 13; hereafter cited in text. See also John D'Emilio and Estelle D. Freedman, *Intimate Matters: A History of Sexuality in America* (New York: Harper & Row, 1988); 171–238; hereafter cited in text.

5. Mary Louise Roberts, *Civilization without Sexes: Reconstructing Gender in Postwar France, 1917–1927* (Chicago: University of Chicago Press, 1994), 49; hereafter cited in text.

6. See Carolyn J. Dean, *The Self and Its Pleasures: Bataille, Lacan, and the History of the Decentered Subject* (Ithaca, N.Y.: Cornell University Press, 1992), 58–72; hereafter cited in text.

7. Louis Martin-Chauffier, *Les Marges* (March-April 1926); reprinted in *Cahiers Gai Kitsch Camp* 19 (Paris: 1993), 42; *Les Marges* hereafter cited in text.

8. Atina Grossmann, "The New Woman and the Rationalization of Sexuality in Weimar Germany," in *Powers of Desire: The Politics of Sexuality*, ed. Ann Snitow, Christine Stansell, and Sharon Thompson (New York: Monthly Review Press, 1983), 156; hereafter cited in text.

9. Quoted in Patrice Petro, "Modernity and Mass Culture in Weimar: Contours of a Discourse on Sexuality in Early Theories of Perception and Representation," *New German Critique* 40 (Winter 1987): 137; hereafter cited in text.

10. For an example of this in urban America, specifically in reference to African-American women, see Hazel Carby, "Policing the Black Woman's Body in an Urban Context," *Critical Inquiry* 18 (Summer 1992): 738–55. Women had been symbols of the city since the late nineteenth century. See Alain Corbin, "Commercial Sexuality in Nineteenth-Century France: A System of Images and Regulations," in Gallagher and Laqueur, *Making of the Modern Body;* and Judith Walkowitz, *City of Dreadful Delight: Narratives of Sexual Danger in Late-Victorian London* (Chicago: University of Chicago Press, 1992). Robert Louis Stevenson called London's shopfronts "smiling saleswomen." See *Dr. Jekyll and Mr. Hyde and Weir of Hermiston* (Oxford: Oxford World Classic, 1987), 8; hereafter cited in text.

11. Mary Louise Roberts uses the phrase as the title of her book on the interwar period.

12. Paul Fussell, *The Great War and Modern Memory* (Oxford: Oxford University Press, 1975), 43. Although class difference often determined the soldier's experience of the war, both elite men (usually officers, the men who tend to be the subjects of cultural histories of the Great

War) and working-class men similarly blamed women for their sense of impotence. Working-class men accused working-class women who took jobs in their absence of being "grave-diggers" and "profiteers." Working-class men's hostility was probably inspired less by the war's failure to regenerate manhood than by fears of lower wage scales (women workers drove down wages), long-standing guild loyalties, and their attachment to traditional female roles as a marker of their own precarious class status. French anarchists and pacifists were particularly hostile toward women, as were German socialists. See, for example, Françoise Thébaud, "The Great War and the Triumph of Sexual Division," in *A History of Women: Toward a Cultural Identity in the Twentieth Century*, ed. Françoise Thébaud (Cambridge, Mass.: Harvard University Press, 1994), 37; hereafter cited in text.

13. Susan Kingsley Kent, *Making Peace: The Reconstruction of Gender in Interwar Britain* (Princeton, N.J.: Princeton University Press, 1993), 31–73.

14. Klaus Theweleit, *Male Fantasies*, vol. 1, *Women, Floods, Bodies, History*, trans. Stephen Conway (Minneapolis: University of Minnesota Press, 1987); hereafter cited in text.

15. His reading of Paris also recalls the woman whose secrets are part of a world of calculated revelation inseparable from court intrigue, what the eighteenth-century feminist Marie-Olympe de Gouges called the "nocturnal administration" of aristocratic ladies. Nicholson does not allude directly to this other stereotype, but there may be another subtext to his allegory of Paris. See Marie-Olympe de Gouges, "Declaration of the Rights of Woman" [1791], in *Readings in Western Civilization*, vol. 1, ed. Keith Baker (Chicago: University of Chicago Press, 1987), 265; hereafter cited in text.

16. In the United States the sexuality of African Americans also undermined conventional notions of masculinity and femininity at this time. In North America race and sexuality are uniquely intertwined and require a far more complex treatment than I can undertake in a survey meant to cover both North America and Western Europe in necessarily reductive terms. The relationship of race and sexuality in the United States has been the subject of much scholarship; studies of the Harlem Renaissance have produced extraordinarily fruitful analyses of this period. The complexity of the topic is rendered with special clarity in Eldridge Cleaver's 1968 *Soul on Ice*, an attempt to celebrate black masculinity without reducing the black man to his body.

17. Dr. François Nazier, *L'Anti-Corydon: Essai sur l'inversion sexuelle* (Paris: Éditions du Siècle, 1924), 12.

18. Robert Bagnall, et al., "Burdens on Gay Litigants and Bias in the Court System: Homosexual Panic, Child Custody, and Anonymous

Parties," *Harvard Civil Rights–Civil Liberties Law Review* 19 (Summer 1984): 499.

19. Ruth Margarete Roellig, *Berlins lesbische Frauen* (Leipzig: Bruno Gebauer Verlag für Kulturprobleme, 1928), 110; hereafter cited in text.

20. This depiction of lesbian sexuality is representative of many (if not all) of the interwar French discussions of the anxiety provoked by lesbians, and in relatively unknown writings by lesbians themselves. Almost no research has been conducted on this topic. See, among others, works by interwar women writers celebrating Reneé Vivien's same-sex desire: Héra Mirtel, "Renée Vivien" *La Vie Moderne: Journal des Lettrés et des Artistes* 31 (July 1910), no page numbering; Camille Arnot, *Des Violettes pour Renée Vivien* (Paris: Sansot, n.d.); Rita del Noiram, *Des Accords sur le Luth* (Saint Raphaël: Éditions des Tablettes, 1920). The number of works of this genre devoted to Vivien is endless.

CHAPTER 4

1. Linda Gordon, *Woman's Body, Woman's Right: Birth Control in America* (New York: Penguin, 1990). Gordon notes, however, that the backlash of the late nineteenth century also produced a new birth control movement in the 1910s and 1920s that advocated the separation of sex from reproduction, women's right to sexual freedom, and reproductive rights. These discourses were gradually appropriated by medical and legal professionals in their own interests (183–242). See Nancy Cott, "The Modern Woman of the 1920s, American Style," in Thébaud, *History of Women,* 76–91.

2. William H. Schneider, *Quality and Quantity: The Quest for Biological Regeneration in Twentieth-Century France* (Cambridge: Cambridge University Press, 1990), 32–33.

3. John Macnical, "The Voluntary Sterilization Campaign in Britain, 1918–1939," in Fout, *Forbidden History,* 328.

4. Cornelia Usborne, *The Politics of the Body in Weimar Germany: Women's Reproductive Rights and Duties* (Ann Arbor: University of Michigan Press, 1992), 109–11; hereafter cited in text.

5. Nella Larsen, *"Quicksand" and "Passing,"* ed. Deborah E. McDowell (New Brunswick, N.J.: Rutgers University Press, 1986), 205. In an earlier passage, two black (one "passing") women discuss why whites go to Harlem: "What do they come for? Same reason you're here, to see Negroes. But why? Various motives, Irene explained" (198).

6. Quoted in June Rose, *Marie Stopes and the Sexual Revolution* (London: Faber & Faber, 1992), 113.

7. Theodoor Hendrik van de Velde, *Ideal Marriage: Its Physiology and Technique,* trans. Stella Browne (New York: Random House, 1930).

8. In Nazi Germany, where they were most ruthlessly applied, the population policies were antinationalist: the ideology of separate spheres institutionalized in democratic countries, which glorified motherhood, was finally an obstacle to the Nazis' desire to annihilate racially inferior women. The Nazis also targeted for elimination all that was symbolically equated with the contagion and fluidity of femininity, including Jews and homosexuals. See Gisela Bock, "'Racism and Sexism in Nazi Germany: Motherhood, Compulsory Sterilization, and the State," *Signs* (Spring, 1983): 400–21; Bock, "Equality and Difference in National Socialist Racism" in *Equality and Difference* (New York: Routledge, 1994), 89–109. See also the debate between Bock and Claudia Koonz, both in *Geschichte und Gesellschaft* 18 (1992): 394–99. On Italian fascism, see Victoria De Granzia, *How Fascism Ruled Italy, 1922–1945* (Berkeley: University of California Press, 1992), esp. 77–115. See also De Grazia, "How Mussolini Ruled Italian Women," in Thébaud, *History of Women* 120–48.

9. Havelock Ellis, The Task of Social Hygiene (Boston: Houghton Mifflin, 1914), 215; hereafter cited in text.

10. Quoted in Ian Hunter, David Saunders, and Dugald Williamson, *On Pornography: Literature, Sexuality, and Obscenity Law* (New York: St. Martin's Press, 1993), 192; hereafter cited in text.

11. Granville Stanley Hall, *Adolescence: Its Psychology and Its Relations to Physiology, Anthropology, Sociology, Sex, Crime, Religion, and Education*, vols. 1 and 2 (New York: Appleton, 1904), esp. 1:432–71 and 2:95–143.

12. Lionel d'Autrec, *L'Outrage aux moeurs* (Paris: Éditions de l'Épi, 1923), 288; hereafter cited in text.

13. Paul Lapeire, *Essai juridique et historique sur l'outrage aux bonnes moeurs par le livre, l'écrit, et l'imprimé* (Lille: Douriez-Bataille, 1931), 23.

14. These movements had their roots in the 1890s. See Steakley, *Homosexual Rights Movement*, 28.

15. Jill Julius Matthews, "They Had Such a Lot of Fun: The Women's League of Health and Beauty between the War," *History Workshop Journal* 30 (Autumn 1990): 48; hereafter cited in text.

16. Anthony Giddens, *The Transformation of Intimacy: Sexuality, Love, and Eroticism in Modern Societies* (Stanford, Calif.: Stanford University Press, 1992), 163.

17. Arthur M. Schlesinger, Jr., *The Vital Center: The Politics of Freedom* [1949] (New York: De Capo Press, 1988), 85, 53, 151. I thank Ruth Feldstein for this reference.

18. Most recently, Scott Lively of the Oregon Citizen's Alliance—a group that has sponsored antigay referenda—claimed that the Nazi

Party was made up of homosexuals (*Los Angeles Times*, 4 December 1994, M3).

19. Alice Yaeger Kaplan, *Reproductions of Banality: Fascism, Literature, and French Intellectual Life* (Minneapolis: University of Minnesota Press, 1986), 13.

CHAPTER 5

1. Daniel Bécourt, *Livres condamnés, livres interdits: Régime juridique du livre* (Paris: Cercle de la Librairie, 1972), 111; hereafter cited in text.

2. The laws under which such materials could be prosecuted originated, of course, in the late nineteenth century, as discussed in chapter 1.

3. Ian Hunter, David Saunders, and Dugald Williamson, *On Pornography: Literature, Sexuality, and Obscenity Law* (New York: St. Martin's Press, 1993), 159.

4. See Stephen Jeffery-Poulter, *Peers, Queers, and Commons: The Struggle for Gay Law Reform from 1950 to the Present* (London: Routledge, 1991), 5–6.

5. Claire Duchen, *Women's Rights and Women's Lives in France: 1944–1968* (New York: Routledge, 1994), 40–87.

6. Robert G. Moeller, "Reconstructing the Family in Reconstruction Germany: Women and Social Policy in the Federal Republic, 1949–1955," *Feminist Studies* 15 (Spring 1989): 137–69.

7. Barbara Ehrenreich, *The Hearts of Men: American Dreams and the Flight from Commitment* (New York: Anchor, 1983).

8. Bonnie Smith, *Changing Lives: Women in European History Since 1700* (Lexington: D.C. Heath & Co., 1989), 510–11.

9. Claire Duchen, *Feminism in France from May '68 to Mitterrand* (London: Routledge & Kegan Paul, 1986), 105–110.

10. Roland Eckert et. al., *Frauen und Lust - Die Inszenierung der Affekte* (Pfaffensweiler: Centaurus, 1990), 93; Eva Dane und Renate Schmidt, eds., *Frauen & Männer und Pornographie* (Frankfurt: Fischer Taschenbuch Verlag, 1990), 25–26.

11. Bettina Bremme, *Sexualität im Zerrspiegel* (Münster: Waxmann, 1990), 117–18, 124, 132.

12. For a detailed discussion of the French debates on Roudy and this issue, see Elizabeth F. Garbus, "Feminine Transgression: Historicizing Desire and Subversion in Contemporary France," Senior Honors Thesis in History, Brown University, 142–43.

13. Linda Williams, "Second Thoughts on Hard Core: American Obscenity Law and the Scapegoating of Deviance," in *Dirty Looks:*

Women, Pornography, Power, ed. Pamela Church Gibson and Roma Gibson (London: British Film Institute, 1993), 47.

14. Jennifer Wicke, "Through a Glass Darkly: Pornography's Academic Market," in Gibson and Gibson, *Dirty Looks,* 68.

15. See also Linda Williams, *Hard Core: Power, Pleasure, and the Frenzy of the Visible* (Berkeley: University of California Press, 1989).

16. Elaine Tyler May, *Homeward Bound: American Families in the Cold War Era* (New York: Basic Books, 1988), 109; hereafter cited in text.

17. Quoted in Marjorie Heins, *Sex, Sin, and Blasphemy: A Guide to America's Censorship Wars* (New York: New Press, 1993), 20; hereafter cited in text.

18. Donald Alexander Downs, *The New Politics of Pornography* (Chicago: University of Chicago Press, 1989), 17.

19. This particular depiction of the white male suburbanite as characterless indicates the extent to which the white, middle-class, heterosexual male is the unmarked sexual subject of *Intimate Matters.* In spite of the authors' admirable efforts to be inclusive, other social groups are for the most part different from or assimilated into white middle-class heterosexuality. This critique of the book has been made in reference to African Americans by Ann duCille, "Othered Matters: Reconceptualizing Dominance and Difference in the History of Sexuality in America," *Journal of the History of Sexuality* 1, no. 1 (July 1990): 102–30.

In other words, D'Emilio and Freedman use white middle-class heterosexuality as a framework into which other forms of sexual expression are eventually assimilated through ideals such as monogamy, companionship, and the goal of long-term marriage. Their work begs the question of how elites constituted white middle-class heterosexuality as normative sexuality.

20. Unlike uses that would be made of psychoanalytic language by anticensorship forces, this usage is incoherent: if nonsexual antisocial behavior is a symbolic sexual act, what is it symbolizing? If it is not, as a Freudian would have it, symbolizing repressed sexuality, then how is it linked to sex? And if it is linked to sex, wouldn't it have to be linked through the idea that repressed sexuality is a bad thing that leads to antisocial behavior—the very opposite of what the antivice crusader believes.

21. John Kenneth Galbraith, *The Affluent Society* (London: Hamilton, 1959).

22. Nicola Beisel, "Constructing a Shifting Moral Boundary: Literature and Obscenity in Nineteenth-Century America," in *Cultivating Differences: Symbolic Boundaries and the Making of Inequality,* ed. Michèle Lamont and Marcel Fournier (Chicago: University of Chicago Press, 1992), 110–11.

23. G. Legman, *Love and Death: A Study in Censorship* (New York: Hacker Art Book, 1963); hereafter cited in text.

24. R. E. L. Masters, *The Homosexual Revolution* (New York: Belmont Books, 1962); hereafter cited in text.

25. Gary David Comstock, "Dismantling the Homosexual Panic Defense," *Law and Sexuality* 2 (Summer 1992): 82; hereafter cited in text.

26. The imprecise definition of the panic is paralleled by the imprecision of all efforts to define pornography, as if homosexuality, like pornography, had so permeated all forms of self-expression that it eluded every effort to pin it down. As Burton Glick wrote in 1959: "The phrase [homosexual panic] is used often in teaching seminars, case discussions, and in the written descriptions of case histories," but it is "doubtful if [any] terms in the lexicon of psychiatry and psychoanalysis have been subject to more variegated usage" (quoted in Comstock, 83).

27. In a case study done in the 1920s, the psychiatrist reported that one symptom of "homosexual panic" was that the sufferer felt "hypnotized" in the presence of a "known" homosexual (Comstock, 84–85).

28. See, for example, Albert J. Gerber, *Sex, Pornography, and Justice* (New York: Lyle Stuart, 1965); Robert W. Haney, *Comstockery in America: Patterns of Censorship and Control* (Boston: Beacon Press, 1960); Eberhard Kronhausen and Phyllis Kronhausen, *Pornography and the Law: The Psychology of Erotic Realism and Pornography* (New York: Ballantine, 1959). Terrence Murphy's *Censorship: Government and Obscenity* (Baltimore: Helicon, 1963), is the only book to advocate censorship. All of the above conceive homosexuality, at least implicitly, as a threat to coherent heterosexual selfhood.

29. Quoted in Morse Peckham, *Pornography and Art: An Experiment in Explanation* (New York: Harper & Row, 1971), 22–23, hereafter cited in text; D. H. Lawrence, *Pornography and Obscenity* (New York: Knopf, 1930), 12–13.

30. Steven Marcus, *The Other Victorians: A Study of Sexuality and Pornography in Mid-Nineteenth-Century England* [1964] (New York: Norton, 1985), esp. 254–55, where Marcus equates pornography, masturbation, flagellation, and homosexuality: "The writers of this literature, like some propagandists for homosexuality, need to reassure themselves that their affliction is simultaneously exclusive and universal. (The adolescent who masturbates and tries to alleviate his sense of guilt by saying to himself that everyone does the same thing is following the same procedure.)" Marcus also notes pornography's "sadness and poverty" (254). The only thing these various tendencies have in common is their presumed narcissism.

31. Freud actually never used the term "vaginal orgasm," although he did insist that the vagina was the "leading erogenous zone" in normal women. Thomas Laqueur has argued persuasively that doctors believed clitoral orgasm was required for procreation until the nineteenth century. See Lisa Appignanesi and John Forrester, *Freud's Women* (New York: Basic Books, 1992), 426–427; Laqueur, *Making Sex*, 63–113.

32. Anne Koedt, "The Myth of the Vaginal Orgasm," in *Radical Feminism*, ed. Anne Koedt, Ellen Levine, and Anita Rapone (New York: Quadrangle Books, 1973), 198–207; Janice Irvine, *Disorders of Desire: Sex and Gender in Modern American Sexology* (Philadelphia: Temple University Press, 1990), 163–64.

33. Through activism and more mainstream lobbying, feminists forced states to rewrite their rape statutes and succeeded in making sexual harassment an issue. They also pushed hard to legalize abortion. D'Emilio and Freedman note that women's rights groups did not address forced sterilization as much as they should have, especially because sterilization involved primarily women of color and women on welfare. In 1973, 14 states were debating legislation that would coerce women on welfare to undergo sterilization (315).

34. For a more extensive analysis of moral panics and their consequences, see Gayle Rubin, "Thinking Sex: Notes for a Radical Theory of the Politics of Sexuality," in *Pleasure and Danger: Exploring Female Sexuality*, ed. Carole Vance (New York: RKP, 1984), 267–319; hereafter cited in text.

35. See, for example, Robert Stoller, *Porn: Myths for the Twentieth Century* (New Haven: Yale University Press, 1991), 225. Stoller claims that pornography is most fundamentally about the "dynamics of rage."

36. Carole Vance, "The Meese Commission on the Road," in *Uncertain Terms: Negotiating Gender in American Culture*, ed. Faye Ginsburg and Anna Lowenhaupt Tsing (Boston: Beacon Press, 1990), 118–34.

37. Alice Echols, *Daring to Be Bad: Radical Feminism in America, 1967–1975* (Minneapolis: University of Minnesota Press, 1989), 288–91.

38. Laura Lederer, ed., *Take Back the Night: Women on Pornography* (New York: Morrow, 1980).

39. Susanne Kappeler, *The Pornography of Representation* (Minneapolis: University of Minnesota Press, 1986).

40. Joan Hoff, "Why Is There No History of Pornography" in *For Adult Users Only: The Dilemma of Violent Pornography*, ed. Joan Hoff and Susan Gubar (Bloomington: Indiana University Press, 1989), 33.

41. Catharine A. MacKinnon, *Only Words* (Cambridge, Mass.: Harvard University Press, 1993), 15; hereafter cited in text.

42. MacKinnon refers to Austin in a footnote and almost entirely ignores all the recent debates about performative speech. She acknowl-

edges they exist but makes no citations—perhaps because her position is not at all compatible with the recent work of John Searle, Jacques Derrida (who engaged Searle in a lengthy debate about speech act theory), Jürgen Habermas, and, most recently, Judith Butler, whose work on "performativity" is entirely indebted to these debates. I cannot account for MacKinnon's refusal to engage in these debates even as she draws on them. In *Only Words* she makes a telling, if undeveloped, analogy between a world "saturated by pornography" and one saturated by "deconstruction" (7); though she never explains what she means by the term, deconstruction is a method of reading commonly associated with Jacques Derrida's work and with poststructuralist thought. I suspect that MacKinnon's analogy has something to do with the fact that both pornography and deconstruction are committed to the decentering of subjectivity, to the rejection of the liberal humanist subject, whether male or female. See Judith Butler, *Gender Trouble: Feminism and the Subversion of Identity* (New York: Routledge, 1990); Jacques Derrida, *Limited, Inc* (Evanston, Ill.: Northwestern University Press, 1988); Jürgen Habermas, *Theory of Communicative Action*, trans. Thomas McCarthy (Boston: Beacon Press, 1984); John Searle, *Speech Acts: An Essay in the Philosophy of Language* (Cambridge: Cambridge University Press, 1969).

43. The best treatment I have seen is Wendy Brown, "Consciousness Razing" [review of *Towards a Feminist Theory of the State* by Catharine MacKinnon], *The Nation* (January 1990): 61–64.

44. Catharine MacKinnon, *Towards a Feminist Theory of the State* (Cambridge, Mass.: Harvard University Press, 1989), 197; hereafter cited in text.

45. Corrine Sweet, "Pornography and Addiction: A Political Issue," in *Pornography: Women, Violence, and Civil Liberties: A Radical New View*, ed. Catherine Itzin (Oxford: Oxford University Press, 1993), 182; hereafter cited in text.

46. Catherine Itzin, "Pornography and the Social Construction of Sexual Inequality," in Itzin, *Pornography*, 70; H. Patricia Hynes, "Pornography and Pollution: An Environmental Analogy," in Itzin, *Pornography*, 391–93; Michael Moorcock, "Working in the Ministry of Truth: Pornography and Censorship in Contemporary Britain," in Itzin, *Pornography*, 543, hereafter cited in text.

47. Ray Wyre, "Pornography and Sexual Violence: Working with Sex Offenders," in Itzin, *Pornography*, 236.

48. See Ellen Carol Dubois and Linda Gordon, "Seeking Ecstasy on the Battlefield: Danger and Pleasure in Nineteenth-Century Feminist Thought," in Vance, *Pleasure and Danger*, 31–49; and Judith Walkowitz, *Prostitution and Victorian Society* and *City of Dreadful Delight*. All of these

treatments indirectly seek to discredit the arguments of antipornography feminists by linking their arguments to the moralizing arguments of nineteenth-century women.

49. Andrea Dworkin, *Intercourse* (New York: Free Press, 1987), 85.

50. See also Janice Raymond, "Pornography and the Politics of Lesbianism," in Itzin, *Pornography*, 176–77; and Gloria Steinem, "Erotica and Pornography: A Clear and Present Difference," in Lederer, *Take Back the Night*, 35–39. As far as I can tell, no antipornography feminist seems to be aware of the fact that "erotica" is a category first constructed by avant-garde artists during the interwar years in order to distinguish, say, D. H. Lawrence's writing from "real" pornography. See Hunter, Saunders, and Williamson, *On Pornography*, 113, 192; and Carolyn Dean, "Pornography, Literature, and the Redemption of Virility in France, 1880–1930," *differences: A Journal of Feminist Cultural Studies* 5, no. 2 (1993): 76–86.

51. This argument is part of a larger effort to understand how and why women's historical exclusion from the full privileges accorded to rights-bearing subjects under the law (the right to control one's fertility, for example) is linked to the difficulty of proclaiming and defining women's desire. In other words, women have sexual desire, but its forms have been shaped and regulated in historically specific terms that render the directive to "take responsibility" complicated at best and incoherent at worst.

Selected Bibliography

Acton, William. *The Function and Disorders of the Reproductive Organs in Use, Adult Age, and Advanced Life, Considered in Their Physiological, Social, and Psychological Relations.* London: John Churchill, 1857.

Albert, Nicole. "Sappho Mythified, Sappho Mystified, or the Metamorphoses of Sappho in Fin-de-Siècle France." In *Gay Studies from the French Cultures: Voices from France, Belgium, Brazil, Canada, and the Netherlands,* edited by Rommel Mendès-Leite and Pierre Olivier de Busscher. New York: Haworth Press, 1993.

D'Autrec, Lionel. *L'Outrage aux moeurs.* Paris: Éditions de l'Épi, 1923.

Barret-Ducrocq, Françoise. *Love in the Time of Victoria: Sexuality and Desire among Working-Class Men and Women in Nineteenth-Century London.* Translated by John Howe. New York: Penguin, 1991.

Beisel, Nicola. "Constructing a Shifting Moral Boundary: Literature and Obscenity in Nineteenth-Century America." In *Cultivating Differences: Symbolic Boundaries and the Making of Inequality,* edited by Michèle Lamont and Marcel Fournier. Chicago: University of Chicago Press, 1992.

Benjamin, Jessica. *The Bonds of Love: Psychoanalysis, Feminism, and the Problem of Domination.* New York: Pantheon, 1988.

Bérubé, Allan. *Coming out under Fire: The History of Gay Men and Women in World War II.* New York: Plume, 1991.

Birken, Lawrence. *Consuming Desire: Sexual Science and the Emergence of a Culture of Abundance, 1871–1914.* Ithaca, N.Y.: Cornell University Press, 1988.

Bock, Gisela. "Racism and Sexism in Nazi Germany: Motherhood, Compulsory Sterilization and the State." *Signs* (Spring 1983): 400–421.

Bock, Gisela, and Susan James, eds. *Beyond Equality and Difference: Citizenship, Feminist Politics, Female Subjectivity.* New York: Routledge, 1992.

Boolos, George, ed. *Meaning and Method: Essays in Honor of Hilary Putnam.* Cambridge: Cambridge University Press, 1990.

Bremmer, Jan N., ed. *From Sappho to De Sade: Moments in the History of Sexuality.* New York: Routledge, 1989.

Bridenthal, Renate, Atina Grossmann, and Marion Kaplan. *When Biology Became Destiny: Women in Weimar and Nazi Germany.* New York: Monthly Review Press, 1984.

Brooks, Peter. *Body Work: Objects of Desire in Modern Narrative.* Cambridge, Mass.: Harvard University Press, 1993.

Brown, Wendy. "Consciousness Razing." Review of *Towards a Feminist Theory of the State* by Catharine MacKinnon. *The Nation* (January 1990): 61–64.

Burke, Edmund. *Reflections on the Revolution in France* [1790]. Edited by Conor Cruise O'Brien. New York: Penguin Books, 1982.

Burstyn, Varda. *Women Against Censorship.* Toronto: Douglas & McIntyre, 1985.

Butler, Judith P. *Gender Trouble: Feminism and the Subversion of Identity.* New York: Routledge, 1990.

———. *Bodies That Matter: On the Discursive Limits of "Sex".* New York: Routledge, 1993.

Carby, Hazel V. *Reconstructing Womanhood: The Emergence of the Afro-American Woman Novelist.* New York: Oxford University Press, 1987.

———. "Policing the Black Woman's Body in an Urban Context." *Critical Inquiry* 18 (Summer 1992): 738–55.

Caufeynon [Jean Fauconney]. *Les Vices féminins.* Paris: Librarie Artistique, 1923.

Chauncey, George Jr. "From Sexual Inversion to Homosexuality: Medicine and the Changing Conceptualization of Female Deviance." *Salmagundi* 58–59 (Fall-Winter 1983): 114–46.

Chavigny, Paul. *Psychologie de l'hygiène.* Paris: Flammarion, 1921.

Cleaver, Eldridge. *Soul on Ice.* New York: McGraw-Hill, 1967.

Comstock, Gary David. "Dismantling the Homosexual Panic Defense." *Law and Sexuality* 2 (Summer 1992): 81–102.

Copley, Antony. *Sexual Moralities in France: New Ideas on the Family, Divorce, and Homosexuality, 1770–1980*. New York: Routledge, 1989.

Corbin, Alain. *Women for Hire: Prostitution and Sexuality in France after 1850*. Translated by Alan Sheridan. Cambridge, Mass.: Harvard University Press, 1990.

Cott, Nancy F. *The Bonds of Womanhood: Women's Sphere in New England, 1780–1835*. New Haven: Yale University Press, 1977.

Crompton, Louis. "The Myth of Lesbian Impunity: Capital Laws from 1270 to 1791." *Journal of Homosexuality* 6, (1980–81): 11–25.

Davidson, Arnold. "Sex and the Emergence of Sexuality." *Critical Inquiry* 14, (Autumn 1987): 16–48.

———. "Closing up the Corpses: Diseases of Sexuality and the Emergence of the Psychiatric Style of Reasoning." In *Meaning and Method: Essays in Honor of Hilary Putnam*, edited by George Boolos. Cambridge: Cambridge University Press, 1990.

Davis, Tracy. *Actresses as Working Women: Their Social Identity in Victorian Culture*. New York: Routledge, 1991.

Dean, Carolyn J. *The Self and Its Pleasures: Bataille, Lacan, and the History of the Decentered Subject*. Ithaca, N.Y.: Cornell University Press, 1992.

———. "Pornography, Literature, and the Redemption of Virility in France, 1880–1930." *differences: A Journal of Feminist Cultural Studies* 5, no. 2 (1993): 76–86.

———. "The Productive Hypothesis: Foucault, Gender, and the History of Sexuality." *History and Theory* 33, no. 3 (October 1994): 271–96.

Degler, Carl N. *At Odds: Women and the Family in America from the Revolution to the Present*. New York: Oxford University Press, 1980.

De Gouges, Marie-Olympe. "Declaration of the Rights of Woman" [1791]. In *Readings in Western Civilization*, vol. 1, edited by Keith Baker. Chicago: University of Chicago Press, 1987.

De Grazia, Victoria. *How Fascism Ruled Women: Italy, 1922–1945*. Berkeley: University of California Press, 1992.

De Jean, Joan. *Fictions of Sappho, 1546–1937*. Chicago: University of Chicago Press, 1989.

D'Emilio, John. *Sexual Politics, Sexual Communities: The Making of a Homosexual Community in the United States, 1940–1970*. Chicago: University of Chicago Press, 1983.

D'Emilio, John, and Estelle D. Freedman. *Intimate Matters: A History of Sexuality in America*. New York: Harper & Row, 1988.

Derrida, Jacques. *Limited, Inc.* Evanston, Ill.: Northwestern University Press, 1988.

Doane, Mary Ann. *Femmes Fatales: Feminism, Film Theory, Psychoanalysis.* New York: Routledge, 1991.

Donzelot, Jacques. *The Policing of Families.* New York: Pantheon, 1979.

Downs, Donald Alexander. *The New Politics of Pornography.* Chicago: University of Chicago Press, 1989.

Duberman, Martin Bauml, Martha Vicinus, and George Chauncey, Jr., eds. *Hidden from History: Reclaiming the Gay and Lesbian Past.* New York: New American Library, 1989.

Duchen, Claire. *Women's Rights and Women's Lives in France 1944–1968.* New York: Routledge, 1994.

Dubin, Steven C. *Arresting Images: Impolitic Art and Uncivil Actions.* New York: Routledge, 1992.

Du Camp, Maxime. *Les Convulsions de Paris.* Paris: Hachette, 1879.

DuCille, Ann. "Othered Matters: Reconceptualizing Dominance and Difference in the History of Sexuality in America." *Journal of the History of Sexuality* 1, no. 1 (July 1990): 102–30.

Duggan, Lisa. "The Trials of Alice Mitchell: Sensationalism, Sexology, and the Lesbian in Turn-of-the-Century America." *Signs: Journal of Women in Culture and Society* 18, no. 4 (1993): 791–813.

Dworkin, Andrea. *Pornography: Men Possessing Women.* New York: Perigree, 1979.

———. *Intercourse.* New York: Free Press, 1987.

Echols, Alice. *Daring to Be Bad: Radical Feminism in America 1967–1975.* Minneapolis: University of Minnesota Press, 1989.

Ehrenreich, Barbara, Elizabeth Hess, and Gloria Jacobs. *Re-Making Love: The Feminization of Sex.* New York: Anchor Books, 1986.

Ellis, Henry Havelock. *Sexual Inversion.* In *Studies in the Psychology of Sex,* vol. 1. New York: Random House, 1905.

———. *The Task of Social Hygiene.* Boston: Houghton Mifflin, 1914.

Engelstein, Laura. *The Keys to Happiness: Sex and the Search for Modernity in Fin-de-Siècle Russia.* Ithaca, N.Y.: Cornell University Press, 1992.

Faderman, Lillian. *Surpassing the Love of Men: Romantic Friendship and Love between Women from the Renaissance to the Present.* New York: Morrow, 1981.

———. *Odd Girls and Twilight Lovers: A History of Lesbian Life in Twentieth-Century America.* New York: Columbia University Press, 1991.

Faderman, Lillian, and Brigitte Eriksson. *Lesbians in Germany: 1890s–1920s.* Tallahassee, Fla.: Naiad Press, 1990.

Feminist Review, ed. *Sexuality: A Reader*. London: Virago, 1987.

Ferguson, Frances. "Sade and the Pornographic Legacy." *Representations* 36 (Fall 1991): 1–21.

Foucault, Michel. *The History of Sexuality*. Vol. 1. New York: Vintage, 1980.

Fout, John C., ed. *Forbidden History: The State, Society, and the Regulation of Sexuality in Modern Europe*. Chicago: University of Chicago Press, 1992.

Freedman, Estelle. "'Uncontrolled Desires': The Response to the Sexual Psychopath, 1920–1960." *Journal of American History* 74, (June 1987): 83–106.

Freud, Sigmund. *Three Essays on the Theory of Sexuality*. Translated by James Strachey. New York: Basic Books, 1975.

Fussell, Paul. *The Great War and Modern Memory*. Oxford: Oxford University Press, 1975.

Gallagher, Catherine, and Thomas Laqueur, eds. *The Making of the Modern Body: Sexuality and Society in the Nineteenth Century*. Berkeley: University of California Press, 1987.

Gay, Peter. *The Bourgeois Experience: Victoria to Freud*. New York: Oxford University Press, 1984.

Gerber, Albert J. *Sex, Pornography, and Justice*. New York: Lyle Stuart, 1965.

Gibson, Pamela Church, and Roma Gibson, eds. *Dirty Looks: Women, Pornography, Power*. London: British Film Institute, 1993.

Giddens, Anthony. *The Transformation of Intimacy: Sexuality, Love, and Eroticism in Modern Societies*. Stanford, Calif.: Stanford University Press, 1992.

Gilbert, Sandra M., and Susan Gubar. *No Man's Land: The Place of the Woman Writer in the Twentieth Century*. New Haven: Yale University Press, 1988.

Gilman, Sander L. *Difference and Pathology: Stereotypes of Sexuality, Race, and Madness*. Ithaca, N.Y.: Cornell University Press, 1985.

Gordon, Linda. *Woman's Body, Woman's Right: Birth Control in America*. New York: Penguin, 1990.

Grossmann, Atina. "The New Woman and the Rationalization of Sexuality in Weimar Germany." In *Powers of Desire: The Politics of Sexuality*, edited by Ann Snitow, Christine Stansell, and Sharon Thompson. New York: Monthly Review Press, 1983.

Haag, Pamela S. "'In Search of the Real Thing': Ideologies of Love, Modern Romance, and Women's Sexual Subjectivity in the United

States, 1920–1940." In *American Sexual Politics: Sex, Gender, and Race since the Civil War*, edited by John C. Fout and Maura Shaw Tantillo. Chicago: University of Chicago Press, 1990.

Habermas, Jürgen. *Theory of Communicative Action*. Translated by Thomas McCarthy. Boston: Beacon Press, 1984.

Haeberle, Erwin J., ed. *The Birth of Sexology: A Brief History in Documents*. Proceedings of the Sixth World Congress of Sexology, Washington, D.C., 22–27 May 1983.

Hale, Nathan G. *Freud and the Americans: The Beginnings of Psychoanalysis in the United States, 1876–1917*. New York: Oxford University Press, 1971.

Hall, Granville Stanley. *Adolescence: Its Psychology and Its Relations to Physiology, Anthropology, Sociology, Sex, Crime, Religion, and Education*. Vols. 1 and 2. New York: D. Appleton & Co., 1904.

Hall, Radclyffe. *The Well of Loneliness* [1928]. New York: Anchor Books, 1990.

Halperin, David M. *One Hundred Years of Homosexuality and Other Essays on Greek Love*. New York: Routledge, 1990.

Haney, Robert W. *Comstockery in America: Patterns of Censorship and Control*. Boston: Beacon Press, 1960.

Harsin, Jill. *Policing Prostitution in Nineteenth-Century Paris*. Princeton, N.J.: Princeton University Press, 1985.

Heins, Marjorie. *Sex, Sin, and Blasphemy: A Guide to America's Censorship Wars*. New York: New Press, 1993.

Herdt, Gilbert, ed. *Third Sex, Third Gender: Beyond Sexual Dimorphism in Culture and History*. New York: Zone Books, 1994.

Hirschfeld, Magnus. *Berlins Dritte Geschlecht, Schwule und Lesben um 1900* [1905]. Berlin: Verlag Rosa Winkel, 1991.

Hobson, Barbara Meil. *Uneasy Virtue: The Politics of Prostitution and the American Reform Tradition*. Chicago: University of Chicago Press, 1987.

Hoff, Joan. "Why Is There No History of Pornography?" In *For Adult Users Only: The Dilemma of Violent Pornography*, edited by Joan Hoff and Susan Gubar. Bloomington: Indiana University Press, 1989.

Hunt, Lynn, ed. *Eroticism and the Body Politic*. Baltimore: Johns Hopkins University Press, 1991.

———. *The Invention of Pornography: Obscenity and the Origins of Modernity, 1500–1800*. New York: Zone Books, 1993.

Hunter, Ian, David Saunders, and Dugald Williamson. *On Pornography:*

Literature, Sexuality, and Obscenity Law. New York: St. Martin's Press, 1993.

Huyssen, Andreas. *After the Great Divide: Modernism, Mass Culture, Postmodernism*. Bloomington: Indiana University Press, 1986.

Hyde, H. Montgomery. *The Love That Dared Not Speak Its Name: A Candid History of Homosexuality in Britain*. Boston: Little, Brown and Co., 1970.

Irvine, Janice. *Disorders of Desire: Sex and Gender in Modern American Sexology*. Philadelphia: Temple University Press, 1990.

Itzin, Catherine, ed. *Pornography: Women, Violence, and Civil Liberties: A Radical New View*. Oxford: Oxford University Press, 1993.

Jacobs, Harriet. *Incidents in the Life of a Slave Girl*. Edited by L. Maria Child and Jean Fagin Yellin. Cambridge, Mass.: Harvard University Press, 1987.

Jeffery-Poulter, Stephen. *Peers, Queers, and Commons: The Struggle for Gay Law Reform from 1950 to the Present*. New York: Routledge, 1991.

Kaplan, Alice Yaeger. *Reproductions of Banality: Fascism, Literature, and French Intellectual Life*. Minneapolis: University of Minnesota Press, 1986.

Kappeler, Susanne. *The Pornography of Representation*. Minneapolis: University of Minnesota Press, 1986.

Katz, Jonathan N. *The Gay-Lesbian Almanac*. New York: Harper & Row, 1983.

Kendrick, Walter. *The Secret Museum: Pornography in Modern Culture*. New York: Viking Penguin, 1987.

Kent, Susan Kingsley. *Making Peace: The Reconstruction of Gender in Interwar Britain*. Princeton, N.J.: Princeton University Press, 1993.

Koedt, Anne. "The Myth of the Vaginal Orgasm." In *Radical Feminism*, edited by Anne Koedt, Ellen Levine, and Anita Rapone. New York: Quadrangle Books, 1973.

Koonz, Claudia. *Mothers in the Fatherland: Women, the Family, and Nazi Politics*. New York: St. Martin's Press, 1987.

Koven, Seth, and Sonya Michel, eds. *Mothers of a New World: Maternalist Politics and the Origins of Welfare States*. New York: Routledge, 1993.

Krafft-Ebing, Richard von. *Psychopathia Sexualis*. Translated by Harry E. Wedeck. New York: Putnam, 1965.

Kronhausen, Eberhard, and Phyllis Kronhausen. *Pornography and the*

Law: The Psychology of Erotic Realism and Pornography. New York: Ballantine, 1959.

LaCapra, Dominick. *"Madame Bovary" on Trial*. Ithaca, N.Y.: Cornell University Press, 1982.

Lapeire, Paul. *Essai juridique et historique sur l'outrage aux bonnes moeurs par le livre, l'écrit, et l'imprimé*. Lille: Douriez-Bataille, 1931.

Laqueur, Thomas. *Making Sex: Body and Gender from the Greeks to Freud*. Cambridge, Mass.: Harvard University Press, 1990.

Larsen, Nella. *"Quicksand" and "Passing"*. Edited by Deborah E. McDowell. New Brunswick, N.J.: Rutgers University Press, 1986.

Lawrence, D. H. *Pornography and Obscenity*. London: Faber & Faber, 1929.

Lederer, Laura, ed. *Take Back the Night: Women on Pornography*. New York: Morrow, 1980.

Leed, Eric J. *No Man's Land: Combat and Identity in World War I*. New York: Cambridge University Press, 1979.

Legman, G. *Love and Death: A Study in Censorship*. New York: Hacker Art Book, 1963.

Loth, David. *The Erotic in Literature*. New York: Dorset Press, 1961.

MacKinnon, Catharine A. *Feminism Unmodified: Discourses on Life and Law*. Cambridge, Mass.: Harvard University Press, 1987.

———. *Towards a Feminist Theory of the State*. Cambridge, Mass.: Harvard University Press, 1989.

———. "Does Sexuality Have a History?" In *Discourses of Sexuality from Aristotle to AIDS*, edited by Domna C. Stanton. Ann Arbor: University of Michigan Press, 1992.

———. *Only Words*. Cambridge, Mass.: Harvard University Press, 1993.

Manning, Susan. *Ecstacy and the Demon: Feminism and Nationalism in the Dances of Mary Wigman*. Berkeley: University of California Press, 1993.

Marcus, Steven. *The Other Victorians: A Study of Sexuality and Pornography in Mid-Nineteenth-Century England*. New York: Norton, 1985.

Mason, Michael. *The Making of Victorian Sexuality*. Oxford: Oxford University Press, 1994.

Martin-Chauffier, Louis. *Les Marges* (March-April 1926). Reprinted in *Cahiers Gai Kitsch Camp* 19 (1993).

Masters, R. E. L. *The Homosexual Revolution*. New York: Belmont Books, 1962.

Matthews, Jill Julius. "They Had Such a Lot of Fun: The Women's

League of Health and Beauty between the War." *History Workshop Journal* 30 (Autumn 1990): 22–54.

May, Elaine Tyler. *Homeward Bound: American Families in the Cold War Era*. New York: Basic Books, 1988.

McCalman, Iaim. *Radical Underworld: Prophets, Revolutionaries, and Pornographers in London, 1795–1840*. Cambridge: Cambridge University Press, 1988.

McLaren, Angus. *Sexuality and Social Order: The Debate over the Fertility of Women and Workers in France, 1770–1920*. New York: Holmes & Meier Publishers, 1983.

———. *A Prescription for Murder: The Victorian Serial Killings of Dr. Thomas Neill Cream*. Chicago: University of Chicago Press, 1993.

Michéa, C. F. "Des déviations maldives de l'appétit vénérien." *Union Médicale*, 17 July 1849.

Mison, Robert B. "Homophobia in Manslaughter: The Homosexual Advance as Insufficient Provocation." *California Law Review* 80, no. 1 (January 1992): 133–78.

Moeller, Robert G. *Protecting Motherhood: Women and the Family in the Politics of Postwar West Germany*. Berkeley: University of California Press, 1993.

Moll, Albert. *Untersuchungen über die Libido sexualis*. Berlin: Fischers Medicin, 1897.

Mosse, George L. *Nationalism and Sexuality: Respectability and Abnormal Sexuality in Modern Europe*. New York: H. Fertig, 1985.

Murphy, Terrence J. *Censorship: Government and Obscenity*. Baltimore: Helicon, 1963.

Musset, Alfred de. *Gamiani, ou, Deux nuits d'excès*. Paris: L'Or du Temps, 1970.

Nead, Lynda. *Myths of Sexuality: Representations of Women in Victorian Britain*. Oxford: Blackwell, 1988.

Nolte, Ernst. *Three Faces of Fascism: Action Française, Italian Fascism, National Socialism*. Translated by Leila Vennewitz. New York: New American Library, 1969.

Nordau, Max. *Degeneration*. New York: Appleton, 1895.

Nye, Robert. *Crime, Madness, and Politics in Modern France*. Princeton, N.J.: Princeton University Press, 1984.

———. *Masculinity and Male Codes of Honor in Modern France*. Oxford: Oxford University Press, 1993.

Offen, Karen. "Depopulation, Nationalism, and Feminism in Fin-de-Siècle France." *American Historical Review* 89, (1984): 648–76.

Paglia, Camille. *Sexual Personae: Art and Decadence from Nefertiti to Emily Dickinson*. New Haven: Yale University Press, 1990.

Parker, Andrew, Mary Russo, Doris Sommer, and Patricia Yaeger, eds. *Nationalisms and Sexualities*. New York: Routledge, 1992.

Paul, G. St. *Thèmes psychologiques: Invertis et homosexuels*. Paris: Vigot Frères, 1930.

Peckham, Morse. *Pornography and Art: An Experiment in Explanation*. New York: Harper & Row, 1971.

Peiss, Kathy, Christina Simmons, and Robert A. Padgug, eds. *Passion and Power: Sexuality in History*. Philadelphia: Temple University Press, 1989.

Petro, Patrice. "Modernity and Mass Culture in Weimar: Contours of a Discourse on Sexuality in Early Theories of Perception and Representation." *New German Critique* 40 (Winter 1987): 115–46.

Plant, Richard. *The Pink Triangle: The Nazi War against Homosexuals*. New York: Henry Holt, 1986.

Randall, Jane, and Susan Mendus, eds. *Sexuality and Subordination: Interdisciplinary Studies of Gender in the Nineteenth Century*. New York: Routledge, 1989.

Reich, Wilhelm. *SexPol: Essays, 1929–1934*. Translated and edited by Lee Baxandall. New York: Vintage, 1972.

Roberts, Mary Louise. *Civilization without Sexes: Reconstructing Gender in Postwar France, 1917–1927*. Chicago: University of Chicago Press, 1994.

Robinson, Paul. *The Modernization of Sex: Havelock Ellis, Alfred Kinsey, William Masters, and Virginia Johnson*. Ithaca, N.Y.: Cornell University Press, 1989.

Roellig, Ruth Margarete. *Berlins lesbiche Frauen*. Leipzig: Bruno Gebauer Verlag für Kulturprobleme, 1928.

Roiphe, Katie. *The Morning After: Sex, Fear, and Feminism on Campus*. Boston: Little, Brown and Co., 1993.

Rose, June. *Marie Stopes and the Sexual Revolution*. London: Faber & Faber, 1992.

Rosen, Ruth. *The Lost Sisterhood: Prostitution in America 1900–1918*. Baltimore: Johns Hopkins University Press, 1982.

Ross, Andrew. *Intellectuals and Popular Culture*. New York: Routledge, 1989.

Roux, Joanny. *Psychologie de l'instinct sexuel*. Paris: J. B. Ballière et Fils, 1899.

Russet, Cynthia Eagle. *Sexual Science: The Victorian Construction of Womanhood*. Cambridge, Mass.: Harvard University Press, 1989.

"Dr. Samuel." *La Flagellation dans les maisons de tolérance*. Paris: Maurice Wandnoël, n.d.

Schiebinger, Londa L. *The Mind Has No Sex? Women in the Origins of Modern Science*. Cambridge, Mass.: Harvard University Press, 1989.

Schneider, William H. *Quality and Quantity: The Quest for Biological Regeneration in Twentieth-Century France*. Cambridge: Cambridge University Press, 1990.

Searle, John R. *Speech Acts: An Essay in the Philosophy of Language*. Cambridge: Cambridge University Press, 1969.

Sedgwick, Eve Kosofsky. *Epistemology of the Closet*. Berkeley: University of California Press, 1990.

Segal, Lynne, and Mary McIntosh. *Sex Exposed: Sexuality and the Pornography Debate*. New Brunswick, N.J.: Rutgers University Press, 1993.

Seidman, Steven. "The Power of Desire and the Danger of Pleasure: Victorian Sexuality Reconsidered." *Journal of Social History* 1, (1990): 47–67.

———. *Embattled Eros: Sexual Politics and Ethics in Contemporary America*. New York: Routledge, 1992.

Shapiro, Ann-Louise. "Love Stories: Female Crimes of Passion in Fin-de-Siècle Paris." *differences: A Journal of Feminist Cultural Studies* 3, no. 3 (1991): 45–68.

Smart, Carol, ed. *Regulating Womanhood: Historical Essays on Marriage, Motherhood, and Sexuality*. New York: Routledge, 1992.

Smith, Bonnie. *Changing Lives: Women in European Culture since 1700*. New York: Heath, 1989.

Smith-Rosenberg, Carroll. *Disorderly Conduct: Visions of Gender in Victorian America*. Oxford: Oxford University Press, 1985.

Snitow, Ann, Christine Stansell, and Sharon Thomson, eds. *Powers of Desire: The Politics of Sexuality*. New York: Monthly Review Press, 1983.

Stanton, Domna C., ed. *Discourses of Sexuality from Aristotle to AIDS*. Ann Arbor: University of Michigan Press, 1992.

Stark, Gary D. "Porn, Society, and the Law in Imperial Germany." *Central European History* 14 (September 1981): 200–229.

Stoller, Robert. *Porn: Myths for the Twentieth Century*. New Haven: Yale University Press, 1991.

Stora-Lamarre, Annie. *L'Enfer de la IIIe République: Censeurs et Pornographes: 1881–1914*. Paris: Imago, 1990.

Suleiman, Susan Ruban, ed. *The Female Body in Western Culture: Contemporary Perspectives*. Cambridge, Mass.: Harvard University Press, 1986.

Thébaud, Françoise, ed. *A History of Women: Toward a Cultural Identity in the Twentieth Century*. Cambridge, Mass.: Harvard University Press, 1994.

Theweleit, Klaus. *Women, Floods, Bodies, History*. Vol. 1 of *Male Fantasies*. Translated by Stephen Conway. Minneapolis: University of Minnesota Press, 1987.

———. *Male Bodies: Psychoanalyzing the White Terror*. Vol. 2 of *Male Fantasies*. Translated by Erica Carter and Chris Turner. Minneapolis: University of Minnesota Press, 1989.

Thoinot, L. *Attentat aux moeurs et perversions du sens génital*. Paris: Octave Doin, 1898.

Toepfer, Karl. "Nudity and Modernity in German Dance, 1910–1930." *Journal of the History of Sexuality* 1 (1992): 58–108.

Turner, Henry A., ed. *Reappraisals of Fascism*. New York: New Viewpoints, 1975.

Usborne, Cornelia. The Politics of the Body in Weimar Germany: Women's Reproductive Rights and Duties. Ann Arbor: University of Michigan Press, 1992.

Vance, Carole, ed. *Pleasure and Danger: Exploring Female Sexuality*. New York: RKP, 1984.

———. "The Meese Commission on the Road." In *Uncertain Terms: Negotiating Gender in American Culture*, edited by Faye Ginsburg and Anna Lowenhaupt Tsing. Boston: Beacon Press, 1990.

Velde, Theodoor Hendrik van de. *Ideal Marriage: Its Physiology and Technique*. Translated by Stella Browne. New York: Random House, 1930.

Vicinus, Martha, ed. *A Widening Sphere: Changing Roles of Victorian Women*. Bloomington: Indiana University Press, 1977.

Walkowitz, Judith R. *Prostitution and Victorian Society: Women, Class, and the State*. Cambridge: Cambridge University Press, 1980.

———. *City of Dreadful Delight: Narratives of Sexual Danger in Late-Victorian London*. Chicago: University of Chicago Press, 1992.

Ware, Vron. *Beyond the Pale: White Women, Racism, and History*. London, New York: Verso, 1992.

Weeks, Jeffrey. *Sexuality*. London: Routledge, 1989.

————. *Sex, Politics, and Society: The Regulation of Sexuality since 1800.* London: Longmans, 1981.

Weininger, Otto. *Sex and Character.* London: Heinemann, 1910.

Westphal, Karl. "Die conträre Sexualempfindung." *Archiv für Psychiatrie und Nervenkrankheiten* [Berlin] (August 1869): 73–108.

White, Kevin. *The First Sexual Revolution: The Emergence of Male Heterosexuality in Modern America.* New York: New York University Press, 1993.

Williams, Linda. *Hard Core: Power, Pleasure, and the Frenzy of the Visible.* Berkeley: University of California Press, 1989.

Wohl, Robert. *The Generation of 1914.* Cambridge, Mass.: Harvard University Press, 1979.

Woolf, Virginia. *Three Guineas.* New York: Harcourt Brace Jovanovich, 1966.

Index

abortion, 12–15, 50, 52, 67
African-Americans, 3, 36, 74, 95
AIDS, 83
American Civil Liberties Union
(ACLU), 85
androgyne, 24
antipornography movement, 82–96
atavism, 2, 4–5, 28, 44; lesbianism, 28, 44; unrestrained, 2

Besant, Annie, 13
bestiality, 2, 9
birth control, 13, 47, 66
blackmail, 15–17
Block, Iwan, 22
bohemians, 49–50
Bradlaugh, Charles, 13
Brown, Helen Gurley, 71
Bryant, Anita, 83
Butler, Josephine, 11

capitalism, xvii, 2, 34
Catholic Church, 1–2
censorship, 49–50, 56, 63–97;
presumed feminity of consumers, 69; sexual others and, 69; sexual reformers and, 74–77

Chirac, Jacques, 65
class distinction, 3–5, 7, 14–15;
erosion of, 14–15, gender and, 5, 14–15; the poor and unrestrained sexuality; race, 15; working class rebellion, 4, 7
consumerism, 34, 66, 71, 74; women as objects of consumption, 66
Contagious Diseases Acts, 9, 11
contraception, 13, 47, 51, 66–67
Criminal Law Amendment Act, 9
criminality, 3, 6, 9–13; male homosexuality, 9–10; prostitutes, 7–13; unrestrained female sexuality, 9–10

Darwin, Charles, 2
De Gaulle, General Charles, 66
degeneracy, 8, 22, 56
democratization, 7, 14–15, 34
desire, 2
deviance, 3, 7–11, 15–16, 20, 22 36;
antifeminist backlash, 36; female criminality; legislation against, 7–11
discipline, 54–57; and repression, 55–56
double standard, 11, 67, 71

Dworkin, Andrea, 86, 94–96
Duchen, Claire, 67–68

economic independence, 34
Ellis, Havelock, 8, 11, 22, 24–25,
   53–54
Enlightenment, The, 1
eugenics, 8, 13, 23, 47–50;
   homosexual rights and, 23

Fabian Society, 47
familial responsibility, 47, 66
family planning, 12, 47
fascism, 53, 56, 59–60, 75–77, 79
female sexuality; "bombshells," 72;
   Victorian paradox of, 6–7;
   unrestrained, 2–4, 61, 72
feminine mystery, 42–43
feminism, 65–74; allied with
   working–class parties, 65;
   antipornography movement and,
   82–97; discourses about sexuality,
   65–69; individual rights focus, 65
feminists, 11, 26; antipornography
   feminists, 82–97
and lesbians, 26; Victorian, 11
fertility, 12
First Amendment, 71, 85, 91
flapper, 46
Focault, Michel, xvi, 2; *The History of
   Sexuality*, xvi
French Revolution, 1, 4, 61
Freud, Sigmund, xvi, 21, 25

garçonne, 38, 44
gender, xv, xvii, 2, 5, 14–15; class
   and, 5; erosion of ideology, 14–15;
   idealogy, 2; public vs. private
   realm, 2; race and, 5; self-
   formation, xvii
gender boundaries; destabilzation
   after the Great War, 37–40;
   lesbianism and destabilization of,
   29–31; erosion between 1850 and
   1900, 8; mass culture and, 37–43
gender roles; private vs. public, 2, 4,
   34, 43, 50; state interventions, 50

Ginsberg, Allen, 74
"good wife," 12

Heins, Marjorie, 85
Hekma, Gert, 19
Helms, Jesse, 65, 95
Helms Amendment, 65
hemaphroditism, 23
heterosexuality; capitalism and, xvii;
   idealization of, 2; transformation
   of, 32–34
Hobson, Barbara Meil, 3
"homosexual panic" disorder, 43,
   77–79
homosexual rights movement, 22–25;
   eugenic movement and, 24;
   protection from legal prosecution;
   23; women's, 25
homosexuality, xvi, 2, 6–7, 9–10,
   13–14, 16, 43–45, 59–61; blackmail,
   16–17; congenital vs. acquired,
   22–23; criminalization of male,
   9–10; demonization of, 77–79;
   disease model, 24; fascism and,
   59–60, 75–77, 79; female, 6–7,
   25–31, 43; obscenity legislation
   and, 65, 72–97; repression and,
   76–77; sexual reformers and,
   77–79; superiority of male, 23
Hyde Amendment, 83
hygiene movements, 47–50

incest, 10

Joan of Arc, 93

Kaan, Heinrich, 19
Kappeler, Susanne, 87
Kemp, Edward, 43
Kertbeny, Karl Maria, 22
Kinsey, Alfred, 71
Krafft-Ebing, Richard von, xvi,
   19–20, 22, 24, 26

Labor organization, 4, 7, 15
Labouchère Amendment, 9–10
Lawrence, D. H., 54, 80

legislation; antifeminist backlash, 36
  sexual regulation, xvi–xvii, 4,
  7–13, 36; "social purity
  movements, 8–11
lesbianism, 6–7, 25–31, 36–37, 44, 83;
  acquired, 44; censhorship and, 83;
  congenital, 44; contagiousness of,
  44; female friendships and, 36;
  Victorian conceptions of
  aggressiveness and passivity of,
  6–7
libido, 4, 19
loneliness, 33–34

MacKinnon, Catherine, 88–90, 94–96
manhood; identified with public
  sphere, 2; legislation and, 10;
  Victorian definition, 2
Margueritte, Victor 37; *La Garçonne*,
  37
marriage, 30, 34; changing character
  of, 34
mass culture, 7, 9, 34, 38–39;
  conceptions of gender, 34; women
  as allegories for, 38
Masters, R. E., 77–79
Masters, William and Virgina
  Johnson, 51, 82
masturbation, 2, 4, 6, 17, 19, 79
materialism, 33
Mead, Margaret, 80–81
misogyny, 40
Morgan, Robin, 86
Morel, Bènèdict-Auguste, 8

nation–states; heterosexuality and
  capitalism, xvii; population control,
  xvi
nationalism, 8
Nazis, 23, 66
Neo–Malthusian League, 47
"New Right" Christian
  conservatives, 83
nymphomania, 6

Obscene Publications Act, 13, 64
obscenity, 13–14, 63–65, 71–97;

children and, 73; criteria defining,
  72
obscenity laws, 57, 63–65
Oedipus complex, 25
opium, 14
orgasm, female, 82–83

Parent–Duchatelet, Alexandre, 3
passivity, 6–7
perversions, 20, 55
pleasure, xiv, 1, 45–46, 49–50
population control, xvi, 7–8, 12, 47
pornography, 14, 54, 64–65, 68–97;
  as contagion, 70; and
  homosexuality, 68–82, sadism, 70,
  75, 77–79, 86; violence, 70, 75–97.
  See also Antipornography
  movement
power; white patriarchal, 4; political,
  7
procreation, 54
professional women, 4, 35–37
promiscuity, 37–38
propaganda, 34–35
prostitutes, 3–4, 6–7, 9–11, 19, 55,
  57; erosion between "good
  women" and, 11; female
  homosexuals and, 6–7; and
  unmarried women, 3

racial "purity," 8., 10–11, 48; incest
  and, 10–11; and nationalism, 8;
  and virility, 8
Reich, Wilhelm, 60
repression, 55–56, 74–77; sadism
  and, 77
reproductive rights, 10, 13
roaring twenties, 46
Robin, Paul, 47
Robinson, Paul, xiv–xv

sadism, 70, 75, 77–79, 86;
  antipornography movement and,
  86; repression and, 77
sadomasochism, xvi, 95
Sanger, Margaret, 47, 52
Sappho, 29

Schlesinger, Arthur, 60
self; gender and sexuality and, xvii,
   1–17, 20
selflessness, 32–34
sense perception, 38
sex, xiv–v; terminology, xiv
sexology, xvi, 18–31, 36, 48–49;
   institutionalization of, 48–49
sexual drive; female, 6
sexual equality, 50–54, 61;
   redefinition of, 54
sexual instinct, 19–21
sexual modernism, xv
sexual repression, 2; as Victorian
   sign of advancement, 2–3
sexual secrets, 15–17
sexuality; complicated terminology,
   xiv; gender and self, xviii, 1–17;
   inseparable from culture, xvi; shift
   in history at end of nineteenth
   century, 1; unrestrained, 2–4
"social purity" movements, 7–11, 15,
   50
sodomy, 1–2
Steinam, Gloria, 86
Stöcker, Helene, 47
Stopes, Marie, 49–50, 52–53

Ulrichs, Karl Heinrich, 22, 24
unmarried women, 3–4

Victorians, xiv–xv, 2–17; construction
   of manhood, 2; construction of
   womanhood, xviii, 2, 21; fear of
   the body, xiv–xv; good and bad
   women, 5–6; paradox of female

sexuality, 6–7, 14–15, 30; private
   vs. public sphere, 2; sexual
   repression as a sign of
   advancement, 2–3; sexual secrets,
   15–17
violence, 75–97; repression and, 77;
   sadism and, 70, 75, 77–79, 95
virility, 8–9; garçonne's, 44; Joan of
   Arc's, 93; nationalism and, 8–9;
   restoration of, 55–57

welfare state, 50–54; gendered
   division of labor in, 51; liberalized
   contraception, 51–52; pronatalist
   regulation, 51; redefinition of
   sexual equality, 54
Wilde, Oscar, 9
womanhood; identified with private
   sphere, 2, 34; legislation and, 10;
   Victorian construct of, xviii, 2, 21;
   Victorian ideal of good and bad,
   5–6, 11
Women Against Violence, 86
Women's Christian Temperence
   Union, 11
women's emancipation, 14, 33
women's suffrage, 11, 15
working class, 4, 7; rebellion and
   unrestrained female sexuality, 4, 7
World War I, 34–36; child care,
   35–36; expansion of women's
   roles, 35; propaganda, 34–35;
   women's economic independence,
   34 women's suffrage and, 35
World War II, 36, 59

The Author

Carolyn J. Dean is Associate Professor of History and Modern Culture and Media at Brown University. She is the author of *The Self and Its Pleasures: Bataille, Lacan, and the History of the Decentered Subject* (Ithaca: Cornell University Press, 1992, 1994). She is currently writing a history of pornography in France since 1880.

The Editor

Michael S. Roth is Professor of History and Cultural Studies at the Claremont Graduate School. He is the author of *Psychoanalysis as History: Negation and Freedom in Freud* (1987, 1995), *Knowing and History: Appropriations of Hegel in Twentieth Century France* (1988), and *The Ironist's Cage: Memory, Trauma and the Construction of History* (1995). He is also the editor of *Rediscovering History: Culture, Politics, and the Psyche* (1994), and co-editor with Ralph Cohen of *History And: Histories Within the Human Sciences* (1994). He is currently writing about conceptualizations of memory disorders in nineteenth-century France.